Herbert Puchta & Jeff Stranks
G. Gerngross C. Holzmann P. Lewis Jones

American MORE! 4A

COMBO

Student's Book

NOTE FOR TEACHERS

The pages of this Combo edition are numbered in the usual way in sequence throughout. Where the numbers are different from the original full edition Student's Book and Workbook pages, a second number is shown that looks like this: 23. This is so that the page references in full edition teacher components such as the Teacher's Resource Book can be followed easily.

HELBLING LANGUAGES
CAMBRIDGE UNIVERSITY PRESS
editora ática

editora ática

Diretora-Geral Editoras Ática e Scipione
Vera Balhestero
Gerente Editorial e de Conteúdos Didáticos
Teresa Porto
Coordenador Editorial de Línguas Estrangeiras
Luiz Tonolli
Gerente de Qualidade e Suporte
Beatriz Mendes

Assistente Editorial: Danuza Dias Gonçalves
Gerente de Revisão: Hélia de Jesus Gonsaga
Equipe de Revisão: Célia da Silva Carvalho e Gloria Cunha
Edição de Arte: Erik Taketa e Mauro Fernandes
Editoração Eletrônica: A+ Comunicação

American MORE! Combo 4A with CD-ROM/Audio CD
Hebert Puchta & Jeff Stranks
G. Gerngross, C. Holzmann, P. Lewis-Jones

Direitos desta edição cedidos à Editora Ática S.A.
Av. Otaviano Alves de Lima, 4400
Freguesia do Ó – CEP 02909-900 – São Paulo – SP
Tel.: 4003-3061
www.atica.com.br / editora@atica.com.br

Dados Internacionais de Catalogação na Publicação (CIP)
(Câmara Brasileira do Livro, SP, Brasil)

American more! : Combo : student's book / Herbert
Puchta...[et al.]. -- 1. ed. -- São Paulo :
Ática, 2011.
Outros autores: Jeff Stranks, Gunther Gerngross,
Christian Holzmann, Peter Lewis-Jones
Obra em 8 v.
Bibliografia.

1. Inglês (Ensino fundamental) I. Puchta,
Herbert. II. Stranks, Jeff. III. Gerngross,
Gunther. IV. Holzmann, Christian. V. Lewis-Jones,
Peter.

11-13335 CDD-372.652

Índice para catálogo sistemático:
1. Inglês : Ensino Fundamental 372.652

2011
ISBN 978 85 08 15452 4 – American MORE! Combo 4A with
CD-ROM and Audio CD
ISBN 978 85 08 14808 0 – American MORE! 4 Teacher's Book

Cód. da obra CL 738264

EDITORA AFILIADA

1ª edição
1ª impressão

Impressão e acabamento: Fabracor Indústria Gráfica Ltda.

Uma Publicação Abril EDUCAÇÃO

MISTO
Papel produzido a partir de fontes responsáveis
FSC® C102676

The authors would like to thank those people who have made significant contributions toward the final form of American MORE!:

Oonagh Wade and Rosamund Cantalamessa for their expertise in working on the manuscripts, their useful suggestions for improvement, and the support we got from them.

Lucia Astuti and Markus Spielmann, Helbling Languages, Ron Ragsdale and James Dingle, Cambridge University Press, for their dedication to the project and innovative publishing vision.

Our designers—Amanda Hockin, Greg Sweetnam, Quantico, Craig Cornell, and Niels Gyde—for their imaginative layouts and stimulating creativity. Also, our artwork assistants, Francesca Gironi and Elisa Pasqualini, for their dedicated work.

The publishers would like to thank the following illustrators: Roberto Battestini, Pietro Dichiara, Michele Farella, Björn Pertoft, Lucilla Stellato.

The publishers would like to thank the following for their kind permission to reproduce the following photographs and other copyright material:

Student's Book
Alamy p9 (log rolling contest), p10 (Bombonera Stadium; sack race), p12 (Pilgrims), p35 (writer), p37, p45 (CD: Food Icon; pizza), p52 (whale), p54 (Mardy Fish), p56 (tennis tournament, school fete), p62 (Boston marathon); **Associated Press** p73 (Moby; Menudo; Bon Jovi); from A Step *from Heaven*, by An Na. Copyright © 2001 by An Na. Published by Front Street, an imprint of **Boyds Mills Press.** Reprinted by permission, p46; **Dreamstime** p60; **Getty Images** p60 (logo of Wimbledon); **©Istockphoto** p6 (shoes), p10 (volleyball; basketball), p11, p34 (Philip), p35 (farmer), p40, p49, p52 (salmon), p53 (Arctic terns), p59, p62 (New York City marathon), p63; **Jupiterimages** p9 (fish), p35 (policeman) p39, p43 (George); © 2004 **Mojave Aerospace Ventures, LLC.** SpaceShipOne®, A Paul G. AllenProject, p19 (SpaceShipOne); **NASA, NSSDC** p14; **Penguin Groups Ltd** front cover of Half Moon Investigations by Eoin Colfer (Puffin 2006) p46; Cover from CROCODILE TEARS by Anthony Horowitz. Used by permission of Philomel Books, a division of **Penguin Young Readers Group** p49; **Planet Space** p19 (Canadian Arrow); jacket cover from THE CURIOUS INCIDENT OF THE DOG IN THE NIGHT-TIME by Mark Haddon. Used by permission of Doubleday, a division of **Random House, Inc.** p46; book cover of THE LOST ART by Simon Morden, reprinted by permission of **The Random House Group Ltd** p46; **Reuters** p30; **Shutterstock** p6, p9 (street luge), p10 (football; baseball), p12, p14 (spaceship top left), p26, p31, p32, p33, p34 (Mandy), p35, p37 (boy, ballet dancer, army reserve officers), p43 (omelet), p45, p53, p54 (Sheri), p56, p59 (concert), p63 (girl); **Space Today Online** p19 (da Vinci Wild Fire); **United States Library of Congress** p13; **Veer** p42; **Wikimedia Commons** p12 (Mayflower), p22.

The publishers would like to thank the following for their assistance with commissioned photography: Ed-Imaging pp 4, 24, 44; Studio Antonietti p15.

Workbook
Alamy p24 (computer games; dvds), p25, p33 (school fair); cover of *ALL MY LIFE FOR SALE* by John D. Freyer (Bloomsbury 2002) p19; **Corbis** p6, p7; **Dreamstime** p12, p33 (movie premiere); John Freyer, allmylifeforsale.com p18; cover of THE END by Lemony Snicket (HarperCollins, 2006) p30; **©iStockphoto.com** p24 (candyfloss); **NASA** p13; **Shutterstock** p36.

Page numbers refer to the original version.

Every effort has been made to trace the owners of any copyright material in this book. If notified, the publisher will be pleased to rectify any errors or omissions.

Unit	Grammar	Language Focus and Vocabulary	Skills	MORE!
UNIT 1 Football? Soccer?	• simple present, present continuous, and present perfect (review)	• sports apparel **Sounds right** /s/ vs. /z/	• talk on the phone • buy things in a sporting goods store • read about unusual sports • listen to an American's trip to an Argentinian soccer game • talk and write about a memorable sports event	Learn **MORE** through English **Early U.S. history** **History**
UNIT 2 Space and beyond	• past continuous vs. simple past (review) • past perfect • narrative tenses (review)	• travel	• give reasons • talk about your trip to school • listen and find out about *A race to space* • listen to a poem • talk about and write a short sci-fi story	**Check your progress** Units 1 and 2 Learn **MORE** about culture **Trains, planes, and automobiles!** Read **MORE** for pleasure **Far out**
UNIT 3 Shopping	• *should(n't) / ought* (review) • gerunds	• money and shopping **Sounds right** spelling	• say what people ought to do • talk about shopping • read a quiz and talk about your shopping habits • read and listen to find out about Buy Nothing Day • write a letter to help someone with a money problem	Learn **MORE** through English **Space travel** **Science**
UNIT 4 A working life	• *be going to* + present continuous (review) • future time clauses	• personality adjectives	• say what you want to do • talk about personality and jobs • read about a foreign girl living and working in the U.S. • listen to two people talking about their job interviews • write a description of someone's job	**Check your progress** Units 3 and 4 Learn **MORE** about culture **Park rangers** Read **MORE** for pleasure **Omelets and hard work**
UNIT 5 Bookworms	• *so / such* • phrasal verbs	• kinds of books **Sounds right** stress in compound nouns	• give reasons • talk about books • read about the Alex Rider books • listen to teens talking about reading • listen and talk and write about a book you enjoyed	Learn **MORE** through English **Migration** **Biology**
UNIT 6 The main event	• the passive • *make / let / be allowed to*	• special events	• talking about events • talking about permission • read about events in Rio de Janeiro • listen and talk about planning a charity event then design a poster for it	**Check your progress** Units 5 and 6 Learn **MORE** about culture **Marathons!** Read **MORE** for pleasure **Chill out at Lollapalooza**

UNIT 1 Football? Soccer?

In this unit

You learn
- simple present
- present continuous
- present perfect (review)
- words for sporting apparel

and then you can
- talk on the phone
- buy things in a sporting goods store

1 Listen and read.

Emily Juan! Hi. What are you doing here?

Juan Hi Emily. I'm waiting for Pete. We're going to the game together.

Emily Oh, I see. By the way, this is my friend Greg.

Juan Hey Greg. How are you?

Greg Hi Juan. Fine thanks, and you?

Juan I'm fine. So, you're not from around here, are you?

Greg No, I'm from Brazil. We live in Rio de Janeiro, but my dad's working in the U.S. for a year, so here I am.

Emily Greg's living in the house next door to us. He's only been in the U.S. for two weeks.

Greg That's right. There's a lot to learn. Some things are really different here! I mean, what are those things?

Juan These are special gloves. You wear them when you play lacrosse. Have you heard of lacrosse?

Greg I think so. It's an old Native American game.

Juan That's right. I love it. I'm not very good, though.

Emily It's a little like field hockey.

Juan Well, it's not really, but never mind! So, Greg, do you play football?

Greg Yes! I've played football since I was six years old. I'm a striker.

Juan A what? Hey, I get it. Sorry, I'm not talking about soccer, I'm talking about our football.

Greg Oh, American football, of course. No, I've never played it, but I'd love to try. Are you on a team?

Emily OK, you two. That's enough about sports. Let's talk about something else!

2 **Correct the wrong information in each sentence.**

1 Juan is waiting for Emily. No, Juan is waiting for Pete.
2 Greg's dad is working in Brazil for a year. ....
3 Greg has been in the U.S. for a month. ....
4 Greg has seen lacrosse gloves before. ....
5 Juan is very good at lacrosse. ....
6 Juan thinks lacrosse is a little like field hockey. ....
7 Juan has never played American football. ....
8 Emily wants to talk more about sports. ....

Get talking Talking on the phone

3 **3** **Listen to the dialogues. Then read the texts and match them with the pictures.**

1 **Girl** Hello, Steve. What are you doing?
Boy Hi Sally. I'm doing my homework. And you?
Girl I'm at the park.

2 **Boy** What are you doing, Monica?
Girl I'm writing an email to my friend in California.

3 **Girl** Hello, Andy. What are you doing?
Boy Hey, Joanna. I'm waiting for a bus. And you?
Girl I'm buying new clothes for the party on Saturday.

4 **Work with a partner. Make conversations similar to the ones in Exercise 3. Use the pictures below.**

Language Focus

Vocabulary Sports apparel

1 Match the words and pictures. Then listen and check. (Track 4)

- [ ] gloves
- [ ] sweatshirt
- [ ] helmet
- [ ] cleats
- [ ] pads
- [ ] tank top
- [ ] shorts
- [ ] socks
- [ ] goggles
- [ ] sneakers

1 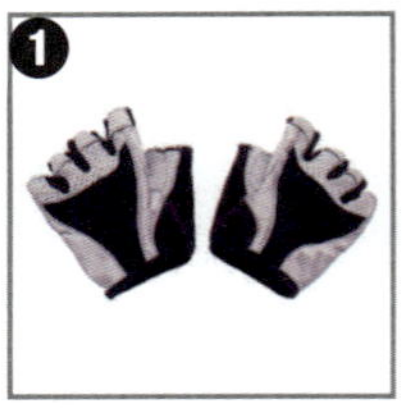
2 

3 
4 
5 
6 
7 
8 
9 
10 

2 Answer the questions about the sports apparel in Exercise 1.

1 For which things could we say "pair of ... ?"
2 Which things might people wear when they:
a) go skateboarding? b) play soccer? c) ride bikes? d) go running? e) play tennis?

When people play ......, they wear cleats / a shirt / knee pads / a helmet (etc.)

Get talking Buying things in a sporting goods store

3 Number the dialogue in the correct order. Listen and check. (Track 5)

...... 10, I think.
..1.. May I help you?
...... Oh, they look fine. Can I try them on?
...... OK. What size do you wear?
...... Sure, no problem.
...... Well, we have these.
...... Yes. I need a pair of soccer cleats.

4 Work with partner. Make similar conversations about:

- a football jersey
- a pair of sneakers
- a running top
- a pair of biking shorts

Grammar

Simple present / present continuous / present perfect (review)

1 **Look at the sentences and write the name of the correct tense: SP (simple present), PC (present continuous), or PP (present perfect).**

1 **Do** you **play** football? ....
2 **Have** you **heard** of lacrosse? ....
3 He**'s been** in the U.S. for two weeks. ....
4 He**'s living** in the house next door. ....
5 I **don't play** very well. ....
6 I**'m** not **talking** about soccer. ....
7 I**'ve** never **played** it. ....
8 We **live** in Kyoto. ....
9 What **are** you **doing** here? ....

2 **Match the questions and answers.**

1 Do you like tennis?
2 What are you doing?
3 Have you finished your homework?
4 What time do you go to school?
5 Do you like banana ice cream?
6 Has Sandra sent you an email?
7 Have you ever been to the U.S.?
8 What are you reading?

a) At eight o'clock.
b) Yes, but I'm not very good.
c) Yes, I'm opening it now.
d) No, but I want to go one day.
e) I'm writing an email to Johnny.
f) A book about Boston.
g) No. I'm still doing it.
h) I don't know. I've never had it.

3 **Circle the correct form of the verb.**

1 **A** Where's Pauline?
B She's in her room. *She's talking / She talks* to her friend on the phone.
2 **A** Are you a good skater?
B Yes, I am. *I go / I'm going* skating every weekend.
3 **A** Can I talk to you, please?
B Not now, *I'm watching / I've watched* a TV show. Let's talk later.
4 **A** What's the matter?
B I can't find my pen. *Have you seen / Are you seeing* it?
5 **A** She likes magazines.
B Yes. *She reads / She's reading* every day.
6 **A** Is that a good book?
B I don't know. *I don't read / I haven't read* it.

4 Match the sentences and the pictures.

1 Paula plays the guitar.
2 Paula's playing the guitar.
3 Alan's talking on the phone.
4 Alan talks on the phone a lot.
5 Our cat chases birds.
6 Our cat is chasing birds.
7 She sings really well.
8 She's singing really well right now.

5 Complete the sentences with the simple present or present continuous form of the verbs.

1 Sorry, I can't talk to you now. I'm having... dinner. (have)
2 In my house, we .... dinner at eight thirty. (have)
3 My father .... home to go to work at 7:30 every day. (leave)
4 Shhh! I .... television. (watch)
5 Do you know where Graham is? I .... for him. (look)
6 **A** I play tennis with Sally every Saturday. **B** Really? Who ....? (win)
7 **A** The football game started 20 minutes ago. **B** Oh? Who ....? (win)

6 Circle the correct verb.

1 Hey, here's the money! I *find / 've found* it!
2 We *live / have lived* in this house for 10 years.
3 Jane's sick, and she *doesn't go / hasn't been* to school for three days.
4 My parents are never here on Sunday afternoons. They *visit / have visited* my grandparents.
5 I don't know what happens in the movie because I *don't see / haven't seen* it.

7 Complete the sentences with the present perfect simple of the verb in parentheses.

1 Sorry, he isn't here. He's... gone... out. (go)
2 I .... never .... to go to Canada. (want)
3 I .... a new pair of sneakers. Do you like them? (buy)
4 .... you .... their new album? (hear)
5 Our teacher .... us a lot of homework for tonight. (give)
6 There are no apples left. You .... them all! (eat)
7 We're still waiting for the bus. It .... yet. (not come)
8 He's nervous because he .... for the exam. (not study)

Skills

Reading and speaking

1 Read the texts. Match each text to a photo.

A

B

C

Unusual American sports

1 Street luge
The luge is an Olympic event in which competitors ride a sled down an ice slide. Street luge is an extreme sport modeled on the luge. It takes place on a paved road and its competitors ride modified skateboards. Street luge began in southern California and the first professional race took place in 1975. This sport is dangerous, so there are many safety rules to help keep participants safe.

2 Catfish grabbing
Catfish grabbing is also known as catfish grappling, stumping, grabbling, noodling, or graveling. Basically, it is catching a catfish with your bare hands. Most of the time the catfish caught in this sport are released. But every now and again a catfish might end up being fried and eaten. Catfish grabbing is popular on the Tennessee River, but also takes place in the southern states.

3 Logrolling
Logrolling is also known as birling. It originated in the northwestern United States. In logrolling, two people stand on opposite sides of a log in a river or another body of water. One log roller starts moving the log by walking, while the other tries to stay balanced. The first person to fall off the log and into the water loses.

2 Read these sentences. Which sport is each sentence about?

1 It's a fairly dangerous sport.
2 You use your bare hands.
3 It started in southern California.
4 It is most common in the South.
5 The loser gets wet!

3 Discuss in small groups.

1 Do you consider these to be sports? Why/why not?
2 Which one would you like to take part in most? Why?
3 What unusual sports do you know of in your country?

Listening

6 **4** **Listen to an American boy talking about his trip to an Argentinian soccer game. Answer these questions.**

1 Which city was Sam in?
2 Which team was playing?
3 What was the score and who won?

7 **5** **Listen again. Decide if the sentences below are T (True) or F (False).**

1 The Boca Juniors play at La Bombonera. T / F
2 The weather was warm. T / F
3 The game started at 6:00 p.m. T / F
4 Sam thought the stadium was quiet. T / F
5 Sam jumped along with the fans. T / F
6 Sam thought the second half was boring. T / F
7 Boca Juniors won the game 3–2. T / F
8 Sam really enjoyed the evening. T / F

Speaking

6 **Choose a sentence for each photo. Compare your answers with a partner and explain your reasons.**

1 Everyone had a great time.
2 We won!
3 It was really exciting.
4 The noise was incredible.
5 It was just for fun.
6 There were so many people there!
7 It was a really important game.
8 We lost but it didn't matter.

A

B

C

D

E

7 **Tell your partner about a memorable sporting occasion.**

Writing for your Portfolio

8 Complete Roberto's text using the words on the left.

country
wait
together
painted
unfortunately
interested
windows
sad

Three years ago it was the Soccer World Cup. I'm not really very [1] .... in soccer, but my sister plays and really loves it. So we had a good time when we sat down [2] .... and watched the games on TV, especially when our [3] .... played!
We were very excited when our country got to the semifinal. And people in our city went crazy, too! They put flags in the [4] .... of their houses, and people wore shirts with the team colors. On the day of the game, a lot of people [5] .... their faces, too. It was great!
We went to our neighbor's house to watch the semifinal. It started at eight o'clock at night. The game was pretty exciting, but [6] ...., we lost 2–1. We were all a little [7] ...., but it didn't matter very much because we all had a good time.
Now I can't [8] .... for the next Soccer World Cup. It's next year!

9 Read the text again and answer the questions.

1 Which sport is the story about?
2 What did people put in the windows of their houses?
3 What did people do to their faces?
4 Where did Roberto watch the semifinal?
5 Who won the match?
6 What is Roberto looking forward to?

10 Write a text entitled "A sports event I remember."

1 Was it a sporting event that you took part in or watched?
2 Where was the event? Or where did you watch it?
3 Who else was there?
4 What was the atmosphere like?
5 What were your expectations?
6 What happened?
7 How did you feel about it?
8 Why do you still remember this occasion?

Sounds right /s/ vs. /z/

8 **11 Listen to some of the words from Exercise 1, page 6. Decide which end with an /s/ sound and which end with a /z/ sound.**

/s/		/z/	

Learn MORE through English

Early U.S. history

Key words

belief	harvest	turkey	tax
successful	native	colony	merchants
fight	corn	independent	harbor

1 Read the article about the Pilgrims. Match the questions and the paragraphs.

a) What happened when they got to America?
b) How do Americans remember them today?
c) Who were they?
d) Why did they travel to America?
e) How and when did they go to America?

THE PILGRIMS

1 ....
The Pilgrims were Puritans. The Puritans were people who lived in England in the 16th and 17th centuries. Many people didn't like them because their beliefs were very different. A lot of Puritans went to live in Holland, but they weren't very happy there, either.

2 ....
People called America the "New World." They thought that America was a place where they could be rich and happy—a place where they could live as they wanted. So some Puritans decided to go to America.

3 ....
On August 5,1620, a group of 101 Pilgrims went to America in a ship called *The Mayflower*. They left England and began a six-week journey to the New World. Many people died on the journey.

4 ....
The Pilgrims did not have enough food. But they were lucky because friendly native Americans showed them how to hunt animals, make sugar, and grow corn. The Pilgrims also found a strange bird that they could eat—the turkey.

5 ....
In autumn 1621, the Pilgrims had their first successful harvest. To say "thank you," they had a special meal with turkey. This was the first Thanksgiving. In 1863, Thanksgiving became a national holiday in the U.S. It is celebrated on the fourth Thursday in November every year. To this day, turkey is normally served for Thanksgiving dinner.

2 **What do you know about the Boston Tea Party? Decide whether the statements below are T (True) or F (False).**

The Boston Tea Party

1 In the 1700s, Boston was a small port. T / F
2 In 1770, North America was still a colony of Great Britain. T / F
3 Americans had to pay taxes to Great Britain. T / F
4. Americans went on to a ship in Boston Harbor and threw boxes of tea into the ocean. T / F
5 The tea on the ships belonged to the British government. T / F
6 After the Boston Tea Party, the British government closed Boston Harbor. T / F

9 3 **Helen, a student, is giving a presentation to her class about the Boston Tea Party. Listen and check your answers.**

Mini-project A moment in time

4 **Write a project about an important event in your country's history.**

Look for information on the Internet or in a library. Write a text that includes:

- A description of what happened.
- Why it is considered so important now.

Use pictures to illustrate the text and present the information in a poster to your class.

UNIT 2 Space and beyond

1 **Read the texts.**

In this unit

You learn

- past continuous vs. simple past
- past perfect
- narrative tenses (review)
- words for travel

and then you can

- give reasons
- talk about your trip to school

A When Dennis Tito stepped out of a space shuttle in the early hours of May 6, 2001, he had a big smile on his face. He had just spent almost seven days in space and had become the world's first space tourist. He had paid $20 million for his trip on the Russian *Soyuz* rocket. He was not the first non-astronaut in space, though. In 1984, the engineering company McDonnell Douglas gave NASA $66,000 to take Charlie Walker, a person who worked there, on its STS-41D flight so he could do some research.

B A space shuttle takes 90 minutes to orbit Earth. In these 90 minutes, daylight and nighttime change for the astronauts. Altogether, 45 minutes of the journey are spent in daylight, and 45 minutes are in the dark. In fact, during a 24-hour period they see 16 sunsets and 16 sunrises!

C Astronauts on the shuttle can choose from about 100 different food items and 50 drinks. However, a word of warning: The taste of food often changes in space and your favorite food on the ground might taste disgusting 200 kilometers above Earth.

D The first people to travel into space were Russian. The first people to go to the moon were American. When Neil Armstrong took his first steps on the moon, millions were watching him on TV back home. Of course, everyone knows Armstrong was the first man on the moon. But did you know that his Apollo 11 mission left a plaque on the moon? It says, "Here men from the planet Earth first set foot upon the Moon July 1969, A.D. We came in peace for all mankind."

E Space travel has always been a dangerous business. Two of the most tragic accidents in the last 30 years were the *Challenger* and *Columbia* space shuttle disasters. In 1986, the *Challenger* had only been in the sky for a minute when it exploded. In 2003, the *Columbia* broke up while it was reentering Earth's atmosphere. On both flights all seven members of the crew died.

2 **Match the titles with the correct paragraph from the text. There is one additional title.**

1 A "day" in space? ☐
2 When things go wrong ☐
3 Eating in space ☐
4 A message on the moon ☐
5 Paying passengers ☐
6 Who owns space? ☐

Get talking Giving reasons

10 **3** **Listen and repeat.**

A Why was Dave so angry?
B Because someone had stolen his wallet.

A Why was Shenna so tired?
B Because she hadn't slept all night.

4 **Work with a partner. Look at the pictures and say the moods.**

sad nervous excited happy hungry bored

A A is sad.

B B is ...

5 **Work with a partner. Choose a prompt from below and act out dialogues like the ones in Exercise 3.**

A Why was George sad?
B Because his friend had forgotten his birthday.

- watch TV all day
- not study for exam
- friend forget birthday
- get ticket for favorite band
- pass driving test
- not eat all day

Language Focus

Vocabulary Travel

1 Match the sentences and pictures.

Minnie is a pilot. Every day she flies from Chicago O'Hare to Washington, D.C., and back.

1 Minnie sets out for work around 5:30 a.m.
2 She gets into her car.
3 She gets to the airport around 6:10 a.m.
4 She gets on the plane at 6:50 a.m., half an hour before the passengers.
5 The plane takes off at 7:30 a.m.
6 The trip takes around an hour and a half. The plane lands around 9:00 a.m.
7 After a rest in Washington, D.C., she flies back. She gets off the plane around 4:00 p.m.
8 She drives home. She gets out of her car around 5:00 p.m.

Get talking Talking about your trip to school

11 **2 Write the phrases on the right under the questions. Then listen and check.**

A How do you get to school?
B 1 ....
A What time do you set out?
B 2 ....

A What time do you get to school?
B 3 ....
A How long does the trip take?
B 4 ....

I leave the house at 20 past eight.

I arrive around ten to nine.

Half an hour

On foot usually, but my mom drives me if I'm late.

3 Practice the dialogues with a partner. Then find out how your partner gets to school.

Grammar

Past continuous vs. simple past

1 **Look at the example and circle the two actions. Which action is shorter?**

In 2003, the *Columbia* broke up while it was reentering Earth's atmosphere.

2 **Look at the pictures and write sentences.**

1 Steve race down the hill / he fall off.

....

2 Jeff cook / a bird fly into the window.

....

3 Oliver fish / he see a crocodile.

....

4 Susan walk on the beach / a wave hit her

....

5 Julia run to school / the clock strike nine

....

6 Lana stand at the bus stop / a car soak her with water

....

Past perfect

3 **Look at the examples and answer the questions.**

A When Dennis Tito had a smile on his face, he had just spent almost seven days in space.
B In 1986, the *Challenger* had only been in the sky for a minute when it exploded.

1 In sentence A, why did Tito have a smile on his face?
2 In sentence B, did the *Challenger* explode as it took off or after it had taken off?

Rule
We use the past perfect to emphasize that one action in the past happened before another.

4 **Circle the verb that is in the past perfect tense.**

1 I hadn't finished my homework, but I still went to bed.
2 After she had done the dishes, she read her book.
3 When James arrived home, he found someone had taken his TV.
4 I didn't buy the coat because I hadn't brought enough money with me.
5 When I got to school, I realized I had left my books at home.

5 **Complete the sentences using the past perfect and simple past tense.**

1 When I .... her face, I knew I .... her before. (see/meet)
2 He .... two pizzas because he .... all day. (order/not eat)
3 I ...., so I .... the exam really difficult. (not study/find)
4 Anna .... home because she .... all her money. (go/spend)

Narrative tenses (review)

6 **Look at the sentences from the text on page 14 and answer the questions.**

A He had paid $20 million for his trip.
B McDonnell Douglas gave NASA $66,000 to take Charlie Walker on its flight.
C When Dennis Tito stepped out of a space shuttle he had a big smile on his face.
D Did you know that his Apollo 11 mission left a plaque on the moon?
E When Neil Armstrong took his first steps on the moon, millions were watching him on TV.

Which sentences contain an example of:

1 the simple past with a regular verb? *Sentence C*..............................
2 the simple past with an irregular verb? ....
3 a simple past question? ....
4 the past continuous? ....
5 the past perfect? ....

7 **Complete the short story using words from the box.**

got	were walking	had left	didn't take
took	had just got in	was shining	were moving

It was a beautiful morning. The sun [1]............. and there was a cool breeze in the air. It was the perfect day for a picnic. Everyone [2]............. into the car. We kids were really excited. A day at the beach and a picnic sounded like the perfect day. The journey there [3]............. long, and we were soon there. We [4]............. everything out of the car and started to go down to the beach. While we [5]............., we saw dark clouds over the ocean. They [6]............. quickly toward us. We ran back to the car, just in time. We [7]............. when the rain started. Oh well, we still had the picnic. A picnic in the car could be fun. Then Mom opened the picnic basket. I looked at her face and knew immediately. She [8]............. the picnic at home!

8 **Look at the pictures. Choose one to create a story with a partner. Then tell the story to the class. Use the sentences below to start.**

As they set out into the jungle, they did not know what was waiting for them ...

As the plane took off, I realized I'd dropped my wallet somewhere ...

Skills

Listening

12 **1 Listen to the radio advertisement and complete the text.**

THE RACE FOR SPACE

Human history is full of stories of explorers who have risked their lives to go places no one has ever been before, from the top of the highest mountain to the bottom of the deepest ocean. Would you like to join them? You can win $[1]..................... million at the same time!

We are offering the Ansari X prize to the first people to build a spaceship that can be used more than once. Interested? These are the rules:

1 The spaceship must be able to carry [2].................. adults.
2 The spaceship must reach a height of [3]................ This height is where a space orbit begins.
3 The spaceship must return with no [4].................. and no injury to any of the crew.
4 A second flight must be made within [5].................. weeks using the same spacecraft.
5 No government [6].................. can be used in the project.

Does that sound easy? What are you waiting for?

13 **2 Listen to the radio news and put a check (✓) next to the correct options.**

1 Which spacecraft won the Ansari X prize?

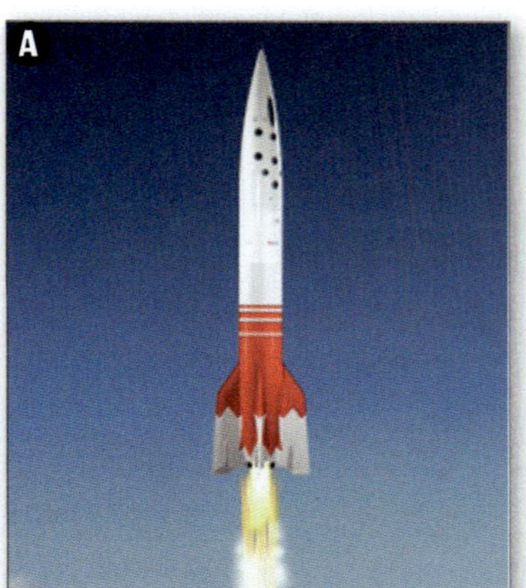

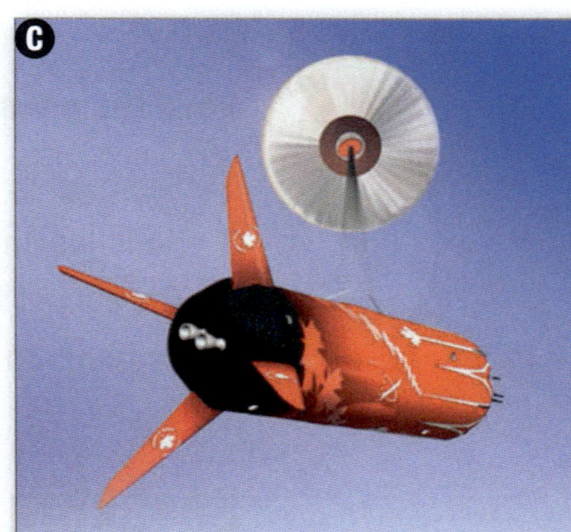

a) *Canadian Arrow* ☐ b) *SpaceShipOne* ☐ c) *da Vinci Wild Fire* ☐

2 How high did the spacecraft fly?
a) 100km ☐ b) 110km ☐ c) 115km ☐

3 When did the flight take place?
a) 10/4/2004 ☐ b) 11/4/2004 ☐ c) 10/14/2004 ☐

4 Who flew the plane?
a) Peter Diamandis ☐ b) Paul Allen ☐ c) Brian Binnie ☐

5 Which company wants to use *SpaceShipOne* for commercial flights?
a) Virgin Atlantic ☐ b) Virgin Space ☐ c) Virgin Galactic ☐

6 How much will a flight into space cost?
a) $20,000 ☐ b) $200,000 ☐ c) $2,000,000 ☐

7 How many people does Richard Branson want to put into space during the next five years?
a) 3,000 ☐ b) 13,000 ☐ c) 30,000 ☐

Listening

14 **3** **Listen to the poem and complete each sentence with the correct word.**

Journey to Mars

I wish I could go back in [1].......................
To a place that I called mine.
Twenty years ago you would find
Life was simple and people were [2].......................

But now the streets echo to the [3].......................
Of so much trouble all around.
Of people mean and [4].......................
Children neglected and needy.

I'm going to Mars
up among the [5].......................
I'm leaving this town.
Letting everyone down.
I'm leaving my [6]....................... behind.
Out of sight and out of mind.

With a [7]....................... and tired face
I travel up into space.
No money for a round-trip flight
On my own, I hope I'm [8].......................
A journey into the unknown.
A new world, a new home.

4 **Read the poem and decide if the statements are T (True) or F (False).**

1 The man is happy because he is going to the moon. T / F
2 He is leaving his family behind. T / F
3 The rocket leaves in a few minutes. T / F
4 He plans to come back soon. T / F

Speaking and writing

5 **Discuss the questions with a partner. Then write a story about the poem.**

1 Who is this man? (Name, age, profession, etc).
2 Who is he leaving behind? Why can't they go with him?
3 Why does he have to leave?
4 Where is he going, and why can't he come back?
5 What is going to happen when he arrives in his new world?

6 **Read aloud your stories about the man in the poem.**

Check your progress Units 1 and 2

1 Complete the names of the objects.

1 football cl _ _ _ _
2 a pair of glo _ _ _
3 biking hel _ _ _
4 swimming go _ _ _ _ _
5 a pair of sne _ _ _ _ _
6 knee p _ _ _

6

2 Complete the sentences.

1 He sets _ _ _ for work at 7:00 a.m.
2 I go to school _ _ foot. It's not too far.
3 We need to get to the a _ _ _ _ _ _ now to catch the plane.
4 When I get _ _ a plane, I'm always nervous.
5 Our plane takes _ _ _ at 9:00 a.m.
6 Did you have a good tr _ _ here?
7 The plane l _ _ _ _ at 11:00 a.m., and we'll take the bus after that.
8 How does your mom _ _ _ to work?
9 How long does it t _ _ _ to get to school?

8

3 Complete the dialogues.

Sam What [1]................ you doing?
Dave [2]................ surfing the Internet. And you?
Sam Not much. I'm really bored.
Dave Why are you so bored?
Sam [3]................ I can't think of anything to do.
Dave Why don't you come over? We can do something together.
Sam Great! See you in half an hour.

Salesclerk [4]................ I help you?
Harry Yes, I need a blue football jersey.
Salesclerk What [5]................ would you like?
Harry This one looks good. Can I [6]................ it on, please?
Salesclerk Sure. Go ahead.

6

4 Write the questions.

1 ....
Yes, I love tennis!
2 ....
Emily's training to become an astronaut.
3 ....
John broke his dad's clock.

6

5 Complete the sentences with the correct form of the present continuous.

1 Sam and Dave .... (talk) on the phone.
2 I .... (try) to help you!
3 You .... (not / listen) to me!
4 .... (we / leave) now?
5 We should be quiet. My brothers .... (study)!
6 .... (she / shop) for clothes?

12

6 Circle the correct tense.

1 I *had finished / have finished* all my homework when he called.
2 *Have you ever played / Are you ever playing* football for your school team?
3 I *don't like / am not liking* many sports, but I *am loving / love* swimming.
4 She *is sleeping / sleeps,* so don't wake her up.
5 What *are you doing / do you do* on Saturdays?

6

7 Write the missing words.

Last week I went to a football game at school. It was a great game and I [1].......... enjoying the action. But then a player was hurt and had to go off. It was bad news for my team because we [2].......... losing 2–0 and there [3].......... only half an hour left to play.

Then, the coach came up to me and asked me if I could play! Luckily, I [4].......... brought my uniform with me. So I quickly changed, pulled my cleats on, and ran onto the field. I [5].......... never scored for my team so I don't know why the coach chose me, but I did my best. You're not going to believe this, but I scored a touchdown! We [6].......... the game and the coach said it was all thanks to me!

6

TOTAL 50

My progress so far is ...

great! ☐ good. ☐ poor. ☐

Learn MORE about Culture

Trains, planes, and automobiles!

15 **1 Read the facts and circle T (True) or F (False). Listen and check your answers.**

1 From 1836 to 1926, a man had to walk in front of cars to warn people that they were coming. T/F
2 In 1962, John Glenn became the first American to circle Earth in the *Friendship 7.* T/F
3 A building where they build airships is so tall that clouds form and it rains inside. T/F
4 The woman pilot Amelia Earhart set three world records for flying in 1932. T/F
5 In 1939, the Graf Zeppelin airship flew nonstop around the world. T/F

2 Read and complete the text using the numbers in the box below. Compare your answers with a partner.

23	1901	1999	three	20 million	2,200

Unusual solutions to transportation problems—past and present

From tuk-tuks to sky trains in Thailand

Tuk-tuks are [1]..............-wheeled vehicles with a place for the driver in the front. People use them for short journeys in big cities in Thailand. Tuk-tuk engines make a funny sound (that's how this vehicle gets its name).
The fastest and cleanest way to travel around Bangkok is by SkyTrain. The first SkyTrain was built in [2]............. to solve traffic problems in the city. It originally had [3]............. stations, but they are building more all the time.

The view from the sky in Germany

It looks very modern, but the monorail in Wuppertal, Germany opened more than 100 years ago, in [4]............., and it's the oldest working monorail in the world. The trains run on electricity, and they never stop due to bad weather. Of course, being 10 meters above the streets, they never get stuck in traffic either! The monorail carries more than [5]............. passengers a year.

The sedan chair

This is basically just a covered seat on two long pieces of wood. One person at the front and another at the back carry the chair and its passenger. We don't know the exact history of the sedan chair, but we know they existed in the Han Dynasty in China about [6]............. years ago.

3 Now answer the questions.

1 How did the tuk-tuk get its name?
2 How old is the German monorail?
3 In your opinion, which is the best way to travel?
4 List the advantages and disadvantages of each.

4 Over 2 U! World cities are becoming more congested and polluted. Work in groups. Design a new eco-friendly form of transportation.

American MORE! Now you can watch Episode 1 of *School Reporters!* DVD

Far out

Emily was a quiet kid. She didn't say much, even to her mother. Her father was always too busy to listen anyway. She never caused any problems. Her grades at school were good. She got along with everyone, so her mother never worried, until the space paintings.

Emily had always loved to paint and she was good at it, too—very good. She spent all her pocket money on paint and paper. She'd started painting when she was seven. At first it had always been animals, flowers, and other things that she saw out of her bedroom window. As she got older, her subjects changed: cars, then people, and then sports events. Nothing strange there.

But then one day Emily found something new to paint. Scenes from outer space. But these weren't pictures of Mars or Saturn and its rings. These were paintings of weird and wonderful futuristic worlds. They showed planets with three suns. And there were strange forests where strange animals lived. Emily's mother had seen the paintings and wondered where her daughter got such far out ideas.

Emily's mother wanted to tell her husband about the paintings, but she didn't. Emily's father was a writer. A few years before, he had written a very successful science fiction series for TV. He was famous and got a lot of work. But now people were starting to forget about him, because he hadn't come up with anything good for a long time. So he had become depressed. He didn't want to talk to anyone, and he often got angry very quickly if someone disturbed him.

Emily was in her room. She had run out of paint, but she had no money left. She couldn't disturb her dad. He was in his office and no one was allowed to go in there—not even Emily's mother. Emily didn't want to wait, so she picked up some of her paintings and set out for the art store. She explained to the owner that she needed some paint but she didn't have any money. She asked the man if he wanted to buy some of her space scenes. He gave her $50 for four of them.

A few days later, Emily's dad was walking past the art store when he stopped and looked in the window. He saw the four paintings that Emily had done. He was fascinated by them. He walked into the store and bought them.

Emily's dad took the paintings home and put them on the wall in his office. He sat down in his chair, looked at the paintings, and started to write. For the next week, no one saw Emily's dad. Day after day, night after night, he locked himself in his office. All they heard was the sound of him working on his computer.

Then one day he came out of the office. Emily and her mother had never seen him so happy. "It's finished," he told them. "My masterpiece."

A week later they were celebrating. The TV studio loved his ideas for his new series and they were going to start filming it as soon as possible. A famous Hollywood actor was going to be in it. The series was simply called "Far Out."

For MORE! Go to www.more-online.com/american and take a quiz on this text.

UNIT 3 Shopping

In this unit

You learn
- *should(n't)/ought*
- gerunds
- words for money and shopping

and then you can
- say what people ought to do
- talk about shopping

16 **1 Listen and read.**

Greg Boy, I'm exhausted! Shopping at the mall is really tiring!
Emily I know. That's why I like shopping online.
Greg Really? You shouldn't do a lot of online shopping, you know. It can be a little dangerous.
Emily I don't think so. Well, I've never had a problem anyway. And buying things online is so easy!
Greg That's true, but I can't shop online anyway.
Emily Why not?
Greg I don't have a debit card.
Emily You should have a debit card. They're useful.
Greg Yes, I know. I am getting one, but it hasn't arrived yet. Actually, it's taking a long time. We asked the bank for it two weeks ago.
Emily You probably ought to find out what's happening.
Greg Yeah, you're right.
Emily Look, there's Juan! Hi, Juan!
Juan Hi, you two. Listen, there's a great new bookstore on 32nd Street. You should go and look around. It has a great secondhand section.
Emily Secondhand? No way! I don't want to buy things that someone else has used.
Juan Oh, come on, Emily. They're books, not clothes!
Emily Well, maybe I'll go, but not now. I ought to go home.
Greg OK, see you, Emily! Now, Juan, where's this book store?

2 Check (✓) the correct answer.

1 Emily likes
a) shopping online. ☐ b) buying secondhand clothes. ☐
c) shopping at the mall. ☐

2 Greg can't
a) spend a lot of money. ☐ b) pay in cash. ☐ c) shop online. ☐

3 Emily thinks that Greg should
a) find a credit card. ☐ b) talk to his mother. ☐
c) talk to the bank about his debit card.

4 Juan has found
a) a good bookstore. ☐ b) a good clothing store. ☐ c) an old bookstore. ☐

5 Emily is going
a) to buy secondhand clothes. ☐ b) to the bookstore. ☐ c) home. ☐

Get talking Saying what people ought to do

17
3 Listen and repeat.

A I don't feel well.
B You ought to go to the doctor.

A I hate grocery shopping.
B You ought to shop online.

A I don't have enough money for a new bike.
B You ought to buy a secondhand one.

4 Work with a partner. Make similar dialogues. Use an idea from column A and an idea from column B.

A	B
I need some exercise.	… go to your room and study.
I'm really tired.	… read a book.
I have a test tomorrow.	… go swimming.
I don't know what to do this afternoon.	… go for a walk.
I'm bored.	… watch a movie on DVD.
There's nothing good on television.	… take a nap.

Language Focus

Vocabulary Money and shopping

1 Read the texts. Who do you think is speaking? Match each text with a picture.

A

B
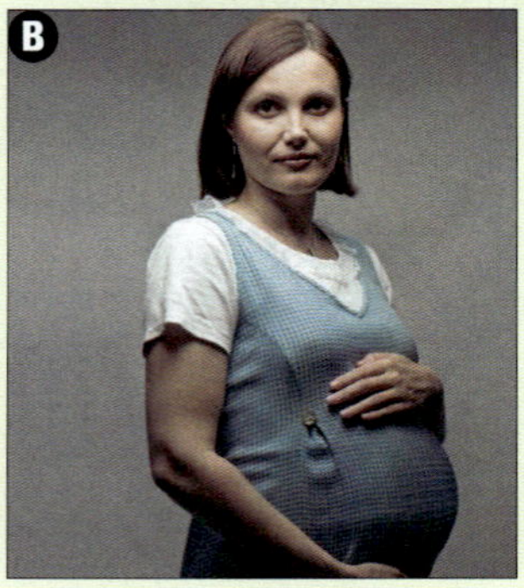
C

We have to be careful with money at the moment. We're going to need a lot of new things when the baby arrives, so we are trying to *save* our money. I don't mind not buying things. It's still fun *window shopping*. When we do buy things, we always pay by *debit card*. ☐

You have to be careful with money when you're a student. When you've bought all your books, paid the rent, and bought some clothes, there's not a lot left. You have to be careful not to *waste* it on things. I usually buy a lot of *secondhand* things. It's cheaper. I always pay in *cash*. ☐

Money? Money's no problem. I make loads of it and *spend* a lot of it, too. I often go on a *shopping spree*. I always buy the best—*brand new* things. TVs, computers, cars. I always pay by *credit card*—buy now, pay later! ☐

2 Find the words in italics in the text and write them in the table below.

Things you can do with money:	Ways of paying for something:	Shopping activities:
You can [1].............. / [2].............. / [3].............. it	You can pay by [4]............. / in [5]............. / by [6].............	do some [7]................. .... / go on a [8]................. ....

Adjectives to describe things you buy:	
[9]..	[10]..

Get talking Talking about shopping

18 **3 Complete the dialogues. Listen and check.**

Only \$1.50 A lot of clothes! Just some secondhand books.
I have been on a spending spree. In cash.

1 A What did you buy?
B 1..................................
A How much were they?
B 2..................................
A How did you pay?
B 3..................................

2 A Where've you been?
B 4..................................
A What did you buy?
B 5..................................

4 Work with a partner. Practice the dialogues.

Grammar

Should(n't) / ought

1 **Who says these sentences in the dialogue on page 24? Match the sentences and people.**

1 You shouldn't do a lot of online shopping.
2 You should have a debit card.
3 You should go and look around.
4 I ought to go home.

a) Emily to Greg.
b) Emily to Juan and Greg.
c) Juan to Emily and Greg.
d) Greg to Emily.

2 **Complete the rule with *should / ought to /* infinitive.**

We can use [1]............... / *shouldn't* to say what we think is a good idea, and to give advice, They are followed by the [2]............... of the verb.
We can also use [3]............... + the infinitive of the verb. We don't use *ought* as often as we use *should*.

3 **Match the sentences and responses.**

1 My room's a mess.
2 I'm not feeling very well.
3 I think we've upset Joanna.
4 It's raining hard now.
5 I get really bad grades at school.
6 Bob's had another accident.

a) Perhaps you should study more.
b) You should clean it up.
c) I don't think we should go out.
d) You ought to see a doctor.
e) He shouldn't drive so fast.
f) Yes, we should say "sorry."

4 **Complete the sentences using the phrases below.**

should go	shouldn't go	should do	ought to buy
should ask	should ask	ought to learn	ought to tell

1 **A** We're lost! **B** You're right. I think we .... someone for directions.
2 **A** I've lost John's pen. **B** Well, I think you .... him.
3 **A** How can I get better grades? **B** I think you .... your homework.
4 **A** I feel terrible. **B** Perhaps you .... to the doctor.
5 **A** Our TV is really old. **B** You're right. Dad .... a new one.
6 **A** I'm going to Peru on vacation. **B** Great! You .... some Spanish before you go.
7 **A** The teacher gets mad at me sometimes. **B** I don't think you .... so many questions.
8 **A** The sign says "Do not disturb." **B** You .... in.

Gerunds

5 **Read the sentences from the dialogue on page 24. Circle the correct verbs.**

1 *Shop / Shopping* at the mall is really tiring!

2 *Buy / Buying* things online is so easy!

6 **Complete the rule with *subject* and *–ing*.**

The Gerund (the [1]............ form of a verb) can be used as the [2]............ or as the object of a verb.

7 **Complete the sentences using the verbs below.**

watching doing playing eating going staying taking

1 I don't like .... in expensive restaurants.
2 .... online games is really boring!
3 .... tests is the hardest thing for me.
4 I love .... in nice hotels when we are on vacation.
5 .... the dishes is the worst job in the world!
6 .... out to the movie theater is OK, but I prefer .... movies on TV.

8 **Complete the sentences with the gerund of the verb in parentheses.**

1 .... old movies on TV is a lot of fun. (watch)
2 I really don't like .... very much. (dance)
3 .... clothes is my brother's favorite thing. (buy)
4 .... my dog for a walk is good exercise. (take)
5 I hate .... late for school. (be)

9 **Complete each sentence using the idea in the picture.**

1 Brad really enjoys listening to music.

2 .... takes a lot of practice.

3 .... with my friends is my favorite thing.

4 My father loves ....

5 .... is the best thing to do on winter mornings.

6 Jennifer can't stand .... in the rain.

Skills

Reading and speaking

1 **Read the quiz and fill in the blanks using the words below. Then take the quiz.**

bought | buy | shopping | save | window | by | cash

Is your shopping out of control?

1 Your grandmother gives you $50 for your birthday. Do you:
[A] go straight to the mall?
[B] buy a DVD and .... the rest?
[C] put it all in the bank?

2 Monday is a holiday and you have the day off school. Do you
[A] go to the mall with your friends?
[B] go out for the day with your family?
[C] stay in and do your English assignment?

3 Do you usually pay for something:
[A] .... borrowing money?
[B] by debit card?
[C] in ....?

4 When was the last time you .... something?
[A] today
[B] last week
[C] last month

5 What do you spend most of your time on the computer doing?
[A] online ....
[B] playing games
[C] chatting with friends

6 You walk past your favorite store. It's closed. Do you:
[A] spend 10 minutes doing some .... shopping?
[B] have a quick look in the window and then walk away?
[C] walk straight past?

7 You need a new computer. Do you:
[A] .... a brand new one?
[B] look in the newspaper for a secondhand one?
[C] see if any of your friends happen to have a spare one?

2 **Discuss the questions and your answers with a partner.**

3 **Look at the key. Add up your score and find out what kind of shopper you are. Do you agree?**

Key:
A answers = 2 points
B answers = 1 point
C answers = 0 points

10–14 points: You live for the weekend and the chance to get to the mall. And when stores aren't open, you're probably online buying things. Do you think it would be a good idea to find another hobby?

5–9 points: You enjoy a good day's shopping every now and then, but it's not the most important thing in your life. Your shopping is under control.

0–4 points: You really don't enjoy shopping at all, do you? There's just one question; if you don't like shopping, how do you ever get new things? Perhaps it's time you learned to overcome your fear.

Reading and listening

4 **Read the text and find out what the rule of Buy Nothing Day is.**

BUY NOTHING DAY

What is Buy Nothing Day? It's a day where you challenge yourself, your family, and your friends to stop shopping and enjoy life. Anyone can take part. All you need to do is spend a day without spending!

The message is simple—shop less and live more! The challenge is to try simple living for a day and spend time with family and friends, rather than spend money on them.

Of course, Buy Nothing Day isn't about changing your lifestyle for just one day. We want it to be something you think about every day. We want people to make a commitment to buying less, recycling more, and challenging companies to clean up and be fair.

To celebrate this year we are holding swap shops where you can exchange your things with other people, free concerts, and shows and, best of all, a cut-up-your-credit-card table. Remember, there is only one rule for this day—BUY NOTHING!

19 **5** **Listen to Mark Goodwill talking about Buy Nothing Day and circle the correct answer.**

1 Buy Nothing Day is:
   A less than five years old.
   B less than 10 years old.
   C more than 10 years old.

2 Buy Nothing Day is celebrated:
   A in Korea only.
   B in Europe only.
   C all over the world.

3 The organizers think that shopping is:
   A bad for the environment.
   B a waste of money.
   C bad for our health.

4 A shopping-free zone is an area:
   A where you don't pay for anything.
   B where shopping is banned.
   C where people do things to get shoppers' attention.

5 To organize a "choo-choo" you need
   A 13 people.
   B 15 people.
   C 20 people.

6 One thing you should do is:
   A give out leaflets.
   B annoy people who are shopping.
   C have fun.

Reading

6 **Read the extracts from the emails and answer the questions.**

1 How much allowance does Sam get?
2 How much was the DVD that Ollie bought?
3 How old is Donna's dad?
4 What is the name of the person in the picture?

...I bought a DVD on Saturday. I gave the salesclerk $10, and he gave me change. However, when I got home I checked my change and I realized that he'd given me change for $50. That means I got the DVD and I'm $42 richer. I can get the money to get a new game and still have some left. The thing is, though, I feel bad about keeping it. It's a lot of money and the salesclerk might get in trouble. But $42 is a lot of money. It could make me very happy... (Ollie)

...It's my dad's birthday on Sunday, and I want to get him a really special present—something to say "thanks" for the help he's given me with my exams. Plus it's his last year in his forties! The only problem is, I don't know what to get him. He loves fishing and especially old books about fishing, but I have no idea where I could find them. So I'm trying to think of something else, but I just don't know what to get him. He's so difficult to buy for. I don't suppose you have any ideas. I mean, what would you buy your dad?... (Donna)

... I was in Top Girl on Saturday. You'll never guess what, but they have some really cool leather boots. They're beautiful. I was going to buy them and then I looked at the price: $99.99. That's almost $100. I don't have that kind of money. I only have $50. It would take me another two months' allowance to save up enough (and that's if I don't spend a penny on anything else). But I want them so bad. They'd be perfect for Molly's birthday next month. Oh, what am I going to do? ... (Sam)

Speaking and writing

7 **Work in small groups. Discuss what you think Sam, Ollie, and Donna should do.**

8 **Choose one of the emails and write a reply saying what you think the person should do.**

Sounds right Spelling

9 **Practice spelling aloud the names of the people who wrote the emails in Exercise 6. Then think of five people in your class and spell their names to your partner, who writes them down. Then switch roles.**

Space travel

Key words

jet of water	mass	force	reaction engine
orbit	orbiter	accelerate	rocket booster
hose	launch	thrust	mph (miles per hour)

1 **Read the text and write three questions to ask your partner.**

How things work: Rocket engines

How do rockets work? Here are a few of the problems that space engineers have to solve when they build rockets:

- What kind of engine can get a rocket into space?
- How will the rocket cope with extreme temperatures? Metal gets very hot at high speeds.
- How can they get the rocket back into Earth's atmosphere?

The engine

Car engines use the principle of rotation to turn the wheels. Rockets don't have wheels, so a different kind of engine is needed—an engine that can "throw" the rocket (a huge and heavy piece of metal) hundreds of kilometers into the sky.

What a rocket needs is a reaction engine. Reaction engines work on a famous scientific principle discovered by Sir Isaac Newton. The principle says: "For every action, there is an equal and opposite reaction."

Let's look at this principle in a simple way. Have you ever seen firefighters dealing with a fire using a big water hose? These hoses throw out a weight of water that produces a force in the opposite direction. This force can be very strong and this is why there are usually two firefighters holding the hose. If the jet of water was too strong for the firefighters, they would go flying back in the opposite direction.

A rocket engine throws mass in the form of a high-pressure gas. The engine throws the mass of gas out in one direction in order to get a reaction in the opposite direction. The mass comes from the weight of the fuel that the rocket engine burns. The burning process accelerates the mass of fuel so that it comes out of the rocket at high speed.

If you have ever seen a space shuttle launch, you will know that there are three parts:

- the orbiter
- the big external tank
- the two solid rocket boosters (SRBs)

The orbiter weighs around 75,000 kilograms when it's empty. The external tank weighs 35,000 kilograms empty. The two solid rocket boosters weigh 84,000 kilograms each when they are empty. But you have to load in the fuel. Each SRB holds 500,000 kilograms of fuel. The external tank holds 541,000 liters of liquid oxygen (616,000 kilograms) and 1.5 million liters of liquid hydrogen (103,000 kilograms). The whole vehicle—shuttle, external tank, solid rocket boosters, and all the fuel—has a total weight of 2 million kilograms at launch. That's 2 million kilograms to push 75,000 kilograms into orbit!

All that fuel is being thrown out the back of the space shuttle at a speed of 10,000 kilometers per hour. The SRBs burn for about two minutes and generate about 1.5 million kilograms of thrust each at launch. The three main engines burn for about eight minutes, generating 170,000 kilograms of thrust each during the burn.

Mini-project Finding out about space

2 **Choose one of the following questions. Go to a library or use the Internet to find out more about it. Write a short text. Add images if you can.**

- One of the challenges with space travel is how to get a spacecraft safely back to Earth. Why is this so? How can scientists make sure that a rocket doesn't burn up under the high temperatures?
- The United States and Russia have had orbiting space stations since 1971 and are now cooperating with other nations to build the International Space Station, a place that will make it possible for humans to stay in space permanently. What will the space station look like? What will it be like to live and work in space? What problems are involved in establishing a space station? What will it be used for?
- Apophis, a 45-million-ton rock, a so-called asteroid, is orbiting the sun at 28,000 mph. If it hits Earth, it could easily destroy a large city. In 2029, it'll be closer to us than our moon is. Find out more about asteroids. What are they? What does modern science say could be done to avoid an asteroid's collision with planet Earth?

UNIT 4 A working life

20 **1 Listen and read.**

In this unit

You learn

- *be going to* + present continuous (review)
- future time clauses
- adjectives for personality

and then you can

- say what you want to do
- talk about personalities and jobs

What do you want to do when you graduate?

Mandy: I want to be a soldier. So as soon as I graduate, I'll join the army. My mom isn't very happy about that. But I'd love to be part of a U.N. peacekeeping force. There are a lot of people in the world who need protection. I'd like to help them.

Philip: I'm going to be a dancer. I know it might seem unusual and a couple of my friends make jokes about it. But it's what I love and there's nothing I like more. My mom and dad are cool about it. They know I'm good at dancing and they know I'm hardworking, too.

Are you doing anything now to help you get where you want to be?

Mandy: You have to be in top shape to get into the army, so I work out a lot. And in about six months, I'm having my first interview to join the army, so I'm getting ready for that.

Philip: Yes, of course. I'm always dancing. I have ballet and tap lessons every week, and next summer, I'm taking lessons in Flamenco dancing. After I finish that, I'll be an even better dancer.

What jobs would you never want to do?

Mandy: I could never do anything that involves working with children. I could never be a teacher, for example. I'm not patient enough. I'd hate to teach someone like me, for example!

Philip: I don't think I could be a doctor or a dentist. I don't like the sight of blood. It's funny because my dad's a dentist and my mom's a nurse.

What's more important, money or enjoying what you do?

Mandy: Money is important. I mean, you can't live without it. But I don't need a lot of money to be happy. I think it's more important to enjoy what you do. No matter what I do, I'm going to enjoy every minute.

Philip: Both are important. Most dancers don't get paid much money, but I'm going to make a lot of money, I think, because I know I'm going to be successful. Am I arrogant? Maybe. Ambitious? Absolutely!

2 **Write *Mandy* or *Philip* in each space.**

1 .... wants to be a soldier.
2 ....'s parents think he/she is making a good choice.
3 .... wants to help people.
4 .... wants to do something he/she is very good at.
5 ....'s parents work in health care.
6 .... wouldn't like to work with children.
7 .... wants to make a lot of money.
8 .... doesn't care a lot about money.

Get talking Saying what you want to do

21 **3** **Match the questions with possible answers. There are two answers for each question. Then listen and check.**

1 What are you going to become when you graduate?
2 Why did you choose that?
3 What job would you never want to do?
4 Why?

a) I'd hate to be a farmer.
b) I want to be a police officer.
c) Because I love animals.
d) I could never be a writer.
e) Because I don't like working alone.
f) I'm not sure yet, but maybe a vet.
g) Because I like helping people.
h) Because I don't like getting out of bed early.

4 **Work with a partner. Ask them the questions from Exercise 3. Then switch roles.**

A What are you going to become when you graduate?

B I'm not sure yet. Maybe I'll be a teacher.

Language Focus

Vocabulary Personality adjectives

22 **1 Complete the sentences with the correct word. Use the people's names to help you. Then listen and check.**

ambitious
hardworking
creative
helpful
easygoing
patient
~~friendly~~
polite

1 Freda is friendly

2 Alan is ……………… ………………

3 Hannah is ……………… ………………

4 Eric is ……………… ………………

5 Harry is ……………… ………………

6 Patricia is ……………… ………………

7 Chris is ……………… ………………

8 Polly is ……………… ………………

23 **2 Match the beginnings and endings of the sentences. Then listen and check.**

1 Ernie does things quickly and well.
2 Ian has a lot of ideas.
3 Keira always has something nice to say.
4 Irene doesn't need other people to help her.
5 Holly always tells the truth.
6 Ralph does the things he has to do.

a) She's very independent.
b) She's very honest.
c) He's very imaginative.
d) He's really efficient
e) He's really responsible.
f) She's very kind.

Get talking Talking about personalities and jobs

3 Work with a partner. Talk about the jobs listed on the right. Use the adjectives from Exercise 1. Say what you think.

teacher
doctor
waiter
salesperson
police officer
web designer
nurse
writer

A I think a police officer needs to be honest.

B I agree. And responsible, too. What about a teacher?

Grammar

be going to / present continuous (review)

1 **Here are four sentences from the text on page 34. Which sentences:**
a talk about someone's intentions? b talk about fixed arrangements for the future?

1 I'**m going to be** a dancer.
2 I'**m going to enjoy** every minute.
3 Next summer **I'm taking** lessons in Flamenco dancing.
4 I'**m going to make** a lot of money.

2 **Match the sentences with the pictures.**

1 He's going to play soccer. ☐
2 He's playing soccer on Monday. ☐
3 She's going to have lunch. ☐
4 She's having lunch with Jimmy tomorrow. ☐

A

B

C

OK, Jimmy. See you at noon tomorrow for lunch.

D

3 **Write sentences.**

1 John / do / homework
John's going to do his homework.

2 Sandra / watch / DVD
....
....

3 They / wash / dog
....
....

4 We / have / picnic
....
....

5 My sister / be / ballet dancer
....
....

6 He / join / army.
....
....

4 **Choose some things to do tonight and on the weekend. Write them down. Work with a partner. Ask and answer questions.**

Are you going to a dance club on Sunday?

No, I'm not. I'm staying at home. What about you?

Future time clauses

5 **Match the beginnings and endings of the sentences.**

A	B
1 As soon as I graduate,	a) I'll be a better dancer.
2 When I join the army,	b) I'll help to protect people.
3 After I finish the Flamenco lessons,	c) I'll visit foreign countries.

6 **Look at the phrases in column A in Exercise 5. Circle the correct words below to complete the sentences.**

1 The phrases talk about actions in *the present / the future*.
2 In the phrases, the verb is in the *present / future* tense.

7 **Match the beginnings and endings of the sentences below.**

1 Please turn the lights off before
2 I'll tell her as soon as
3 I'll leave school when
4 I'll do my homework as soon as
5 He wants to join the army after
6 We'll talk about it when

a) she gets here.
b) this show's over.
c) you go home.
d) he graduates.
e) I get home.
f) I'm 16.

8 **Circle the correct word and complete the text.**

When I [1] *leave / will leave* home, I think I [2] *go / will go* to Canada for a while. Why? Well, I [3] *want / will want* to see the world before I [4] *start / will start* work. I think I [5] *go / will go* to Toronto. My friend told me that if I [6] *stay / will stay* in small hotels and camp sites, it [7] *isn't / won't be* very expensive. Well, I'm not so sure! But I [8] *check / will check* things out before I [9] *go / will go*. But I know I'm going, and as soon as I [10] *arrive / will arrive* in Canada, I [11] *go / will go* straight to Niagara Falls. That's always been my dream!

9 **Complete with *will* (*'ll*) and the verb at the end of the sentence.**

1 I'll call you as soon as I get my test scores. (call / get)
2 I don't think it .... before we .... home. (rain / get)
3 I .... over to your place when I .... my homework. (come / finish)
4 As soon as I .... home, I .... a job in a bank. (leave / get)
5 When my parents .... on vacation next week, I .... the house to myself. (go / have)
6 I .... you back when my parents .... me my allowance. (pay / give)

Skills

Reading

1 **Read the magazine article and find the answers to these questions.**

1 How many hours a day does Lena work?
2 How many days a week does she work?

Life at Camp America ...

Hi, my name's Lena Diekmann. I'm 19 and I'm from Berlin in Germany. I work five days a week at a summer camp in Pennsylvania. I'm a camp counselor. I really like my job because no two days are ever the same. The kids I work with are great and I've made a lot of friends. Anyway, this is my day.

Mornings

I start work very early. I usually wake up at about 6:30 a.m. That's the worst part of my day. I hate getting up that early, but I do it because I have to be awake before any of our campers wake up. I sleep in a cabin with four other counselors. We start work at 7:00 a.m., when we go and help our campers get ready. We have breakfast at 8:00. This is followed by an outdoor activity every morning. Every day of the week we do a different activity such as horseback riding or hiking. I take a break from 12:00-1:00 p.m.

Afternoons

Every afternoon I help teach gymnastics and swimming. I teach gymnastics from 1:00 p.m. until 3:00 and then I teach swimming until 5:00. I help teach kids who are 10–12 years old. Teaching gymnastics is a lot of fun. But I can't stand swimming because the pool isn't heated and the water is too cold! I like to teach though. It gives me a chance to practice my English, which is why I'm here in the first place!

Evenings

I love the evenings, when everyone at the camp eats a meal together. We laugh and talk about the day's activities. Sometimes we have a campfire. We sing campfire songs. Then the children go to sleep at 8:30 p.m. Even though I'm tired, after that I like to sit around the campfire and talk to my new friends.

All in a day's work!

Working in a camp is a lot of fun.

2 **Read the article again and decide if the sentences are T (True) or F (False).**

1 Lena thinks her job is kind of boring sometimes. T / F
2 She likes all the people she works with. T / F
3 Lena sleeps in a cabin. T / F
4 Lena has to work hard. T / F
5 Lena teaches gymnastics in the morning. T / F
6 Lena loves the evenings. T / F
7 She is tired at the end of the day. T / F
8 Lena likes campfires. T / F

Listening

24 **3** **Listen to Kelly and Lee talking about their job interviews. Answer the questions.**

Who:

1 had a good interview?
2 took a dog to the interview?
3 wants to work for a newspaper?
4 has worked as a salesclerk?
5 wants to be a receptionist?
6 wants to start working very soon?
7 said they like working with people?
8 works for the school newspaper?

25 **4** **Listen again and match the questions and answers.**

1 Who is Rover?
2 Why did Kelly take a dog to the interview?
3 What did the interviewer think about the dog?
4 What was Kelly's best answer?
5 Why is Lee happy?
6 What question did the interviewer ask Lee?
7 When did Lee say he could start work?
8 What is Lee waiting for?

a) On Monday.
b) A phone call.
c) Kelly's dog.
d) Your company has an excellent reputation.
e) He didn't seem very happy.
f) Because he had a good interview.
g) Because she had to take him to the vet before.
h) Have you ever worked for a newspaper?

Writing

5 **Complete the text using the words on the left.**

get down
window
wanted
ladder
outside
job

My brother is a window washer. He likes his [1]................... . He likes working [2]................... and he loves talking to people. Yesterday he was cleaning a [3]................... when a woman next door called over to him. Her cat had climbed a tree and couldn't [4]................... . He got his [5]................... and climbed up and got the cat. The woman was very happy and [6]................... to give my brother some money. Of course my brother wouldn't take it.

6 **Think of someone in your family. Write a short text about his or her job.**

Check your progress Units 3 and 4

1 Complete the sentences.

1 We sometimes go w_ _ _ _ _ shopping when we don't have any money.
2 You shouldn't w_ _ _ _ your money on things you don't need.
3 I bought a s_ _ _ _ _ _ _ _ computer because the new ones were too expensive.
4 He won a lot of money and went on a shopping s_ _ _ _.
5 He broke my b_ _ _ _-new laptop!
6 Ian always pays by d_ _ _ _ card. 6

2 Read the descriptions and complete the sentences.

1 She can make amazing things. She's c_ _ _ _ _ _ _.
2 He wants to succeed in life. He's a _ _ _ _ _ _ _ _.
3 John's really relaxed and nothing bothers him! He's e_ _ _ _ _ _ _ _.
4 Anna is always busy and she never takes a break. She's h_ _ _ _ _ _ _ _ _ _.
5 Tony doesn't mind waiting for things. He's very p_ _ _ _ _ _.
6 Barbara always says "please" and "thank you." She's very p_ _ _ _ _. 6

3 Complete the dialogues. Use the present continuous.

A I'm [1]........... (see) my cousin today.
B What time?
A The train is [2]........... (arrive) at 3:00 p.m.
B [3]........... (meet) him at the train station?
A Yes, I [4]........... (take) a taxi there.
B [5]........... (he/come) alone?
A No, my aunt [6]........... (come) with him, too. We [7]........... (have) lunch at The Cedars tomorrow. Do you want to come?
B No, I'm sorry, I [8]........... (do) my homework! 8

4 Complete the sentences with the correct verb or word for the future time clause.

1 As .... as he ....(arrive), we'll go.
2 She .... (leave) home .... she is 18.
3 We will go swimming ....we .... (finish) work. 6

5 Give advice in the following situations.

1 I have to pay a big cell phone bill. (not / make so many calls / cell phone) You ....
2 I want to become a doctor. (study hard) You ....
3 My friend is going to live in Italy. (learn / Italian) She ....
4 I have to get up early for work tomorrow. (go / bed) You ....
5 My brother isn't feeling well. (see / doctor) He 10

6 Complete the sentences with the gerund or infinitive of the verbs in parentheses.

1 I don't like .... alone. (be)
2 There's nothing I love more than .... in the rain. (walk)
3 Gill loves .... (skate)
4 I'm going .... a movie tonight. (see)
5 I want .... a job that involves traveling. (do)
6 Is .... too much ice cream bad for you? (eat)
7 I think you ought .... sorry. (say)
8 Emma hates .... for buses. (wait) 8

7 Circle the correct answer.

1 *I am going to be / am being* a pilot.
2 Mom, *I'm going / I will go* out tonight. Is that all right?
3 You spent all your money? How are you *buying / going to buy* food for tomorrow?
4 Try to come to my party. Everyone is *going to be / is being* there.
5 Read this book—*you're going to like it / you're liking it*.
6 I think you ought to *say / saying* you're sorry. 6

TOTAL 50

My progress so far is ...

great! ☐ good. ☐ poor. ☐

Learn MORE about Culture

Park rangers

Do you know?

Yellowstone National Park is known for its geysers such as Old Faithful, its hot springs, and bubbly activity. All these features point to the fact that Yellowstone is one of the world's largest active volcanoes! But don't fear, the last major eruption here took place about 640,000 years ago.

1 **Read about a park ranger's job.**

Yellowstone National Park
Established in 1872, Yellowstone National Park covers more than 8,900 square kilometers in the states of Wyoming, Montana, and Idaho. Millions of people visit the park each year. It features nine visitor centers and 12 campgrounds with more than 2,000 campsites, and it is patrolled by 49 year-round rangers and hundreds of part-time summer rangers.

Backcountry rangers
Around 98 percent of Yellowstone is "backcountry." There are just 22 backcountry rangers who patrol and maintain the park's many trails on foot, skis, or horseback. They monitor wildlife and help enforce rules and safety regulations with the public who use the backcountry areas of the park.

Patrol rangers
Yellowstone's "front country" includes all its developed areas, including roads. Patrol rangers help to enforce traffic rules. They patrol all the roads within the park and work to prevent car accidents in Yellowstone. Every year there are around 600 car accidents and 100 animals killed on the roads in the park.

Other rangers
Yellowstone also has many other rangers, too. They work in the entrance booths, museums, visitor centers, or spend time educating the public about the park.

Rewards
Many of the rangers who work in Yellowstone only work during the summer months. Few work in full-time positions, and the work is not very well paid. But rangers love what they do. Most would say that they're not in it for the money!

26 **2** **Dick is talking about ranger jobs. Listen and circle the correct answer.**

1 You normally have to have a college degree to become a park ranger. T / F
2 Dick has been a park ranger for 20 years. T / F
3 Dick's first job in the park was backcountry ranger. T / F
4 Dick fell in love with the outdoors on visits to his uncle's ranch. T / F
5 Park rangers rarely work in the same park for their entire career. T / F

3 **Do you have a part-time job? Do you know anyone with an unusual or special job? Tell the class about them.**

4 **Over 2 U!** **Who works in the parks in your country? Find out about their job or another job and write a description. Use Exercise 1 to help you.**

American MORE! Now you can watch Episode 2 of *School Reporters*! DVD

Omelets and hard work: A recipe for success

On his first day in the U.S. in 1990, George Wannous lost all his money. George had left Syria, his home country, because a friend who had moved from Syria to Sacramento, California, invited him to come to the U.S. and work on a fruit farm. But George never got as far as Sacramento.

When the 19-year-old Syrian landed at Los Angeles airport, he took a bus to the center of town so he could get a train to Sacramento. When he got off the bus, a man approached him and took out a knife. He pointed it at George. "The man took all my money, everything I had," George says. "It was awful."

George went to the police and two police officers felt sorry for him. They gave him a small amount of money and put him on a train to Sacramento.

For some reason, George got off the train in San Francisco, and the next day he started to look for a job. First he went to work at a bakery, but at the same time he took other jobs, too. He worked very hard. For half a year, he sold bread in the morning and in the afternoon he cleaned offices for minimum wage. For awhile, he also worked as a taxi driver at night. In 1993, he got a job as a dishwasher in a small café. The manager of the café liked George. He told him to study the menu carefully so he could become a waiter. "All the food on the menu was new to me," George says. "A medium-rare hamburger! In my country we cook everything well-done." George became a waiter, slowly worked his way up, and half a year later he became the manager of the café.

When the owner decided to sell the café, George went to the bank to borrow money to buy it. He started to work extremely hard—up to 20 hours a day! When he was tired, he slept in his car in the parking lot.

That was 11 years ago. George has become successful. He is very smart. Instead of making three-egg omelets as the old company did, he uses four eggs. George says. "My friends told me I would lose money selling bigger omelets for the same price. But I didn't lose money. I got happier customers—and more customers."

George is 39 now. He's happily married and he has three children. He has a much bigger café now, and there are eight people working for him. George has made it, thanks to his hard work!

For MORE! Go to www.more-online.com/american and take a quiz on this text.

UNIT 5 Bookworms

In this unit

You learn
- *so / such*
- phrasal verbs
- words for kinds of books

and then you can
- give reasons
- talk about books

27 **1 Listen and read.**

Juan Hey Emily, I'm bored. Let's go and hang out at the mall.

Emily Can't you see I'm reading a book?

Juan Come on. You can finish it later.

Emily I'm sorry. It's such a good book—I can't put it down.

Juan What are you reading anyway?

Emily It's a book by Scott Westerfeld. It's called *Uglies*.

Juan *Uglies*. What's it about?

Emily Do you really want to know? Or are you just bored?

Juan How can you say such a thing. Of course I'm interested. Honestly.

Emily Well, OK. So it all takes place in the future. All kids are "Uglies" until they're 16. Then they have an operation and turn into "Pretties." Pretties are good-looking. They mess around and have parties all the time.

Juan That sounds like fun.

Emily Yeah, but it's not what it seems. There's this rebel group of kids who run away to escape the operation. It's called "The Smoke." The government is after them before they find out the truth. It's all very exciting.

Juan It all seems very confusing to me.

Emily Yeah, but if you start reading it you'll get into it, I promise.

Juan You know, I'm so bored I might just do that. Hand over the book.

Emily No way. You'll have to hang on until I finish!

2 **Match the sentence halves to make a summary of the dialogue.**

1 Juan wants	a) reading her book.
2 Emily is happy	b) what "Uglies" become after an operation.
3 *Uglies* is	c) take the book from Emily.
4 "Pretties" are	d) Juan should read the book.
5 Juan thinks	e) about teenage life in the future.
6 Emily says	f) the book sounds confusing.
7 Juan tries to	g) to do something.

Get talking Giving reasons

28 **3** **Write the answers under the questions. Listen and check.**

1 It was so good I didn't want it to end.
2 It was so exciting I couldn't put it down.
3 It was so noisy I couldn't talk to anyone.
4 It was so long I slept most of the way.

A How was the book?

....

C How was your vacation?

....

B How was the drive?

....

D How was the party?

....

4 **Work with a partner. Student A chooses a picture to ask about. Student B chooses prompts from the A and B boxes to reply.**

A How was the movie?

B It was so boring that I walked out of the movie theater.

movie

roller coaster

pizza

test

beach

hotel bed

A	B
boring	walk out of the movie theater
comfortable	get a headache
exciting	want another piece
hot	not want to get out of it
delicious	try again immediately
difficult	spend all the time in the water

Language Focus

Vocabulary Kinds of books

1 Match the kinds of books with the titles.

1 a detective novel
2 a biography
3 poetry
4 short stories
5 nonfiction
6 a book about animals
7 a comic book
8 a romance

a) *The Collected Poems of Whitman*
b) *Love in the Spring*
c) *Tears of a Clown and Other Stories*
d) *Ordinary Genius: The Story of Albert Einstein*
e) *Taking Care of Your Horse*
f) *How to Write Better*
g) *The Body in the Library*
h) *Batman Returns*

Get talking Talking about books

29 **2 Put the lines in order to make two dialogues. Listen and check.**

1 A ☐ So what do you like?
A ☐ Do you like poetry?
B ☐ It's OK, but it's not my favorite.
B ☐ I sort of like short stories, but I love graphic novels.

2 C ☐ So what do you like books about?
C ☐ Do you like books about horses?
D ☐ Horses? No, I don't.
D ☐ Football and cars.

3 Work with a partner. Say what you think about the kinds of books in Exercise 1.

4 Look at the books. What kind of book do you think each one is?

5 Which of these books looks interesting to you? If you had to pick one, which one would it be and why?

I'd pick ... because it looks interesting / funny / thrilling / exciting...
I'd pick it, because I like thrillers / love / horror / sci-fi stories...
I'd pick it because I've already read ... by the same author.

Grammar

So / such

1 **Look at the examples and complete the rule.**

*It's **such** a good book (that) I can't put it down.*
*I'm **so** bored (that) I might just do that.*

Rule

We can use [1].......... before a noun and [2]............ before an adjective to emphasize the quality of the noun or adjective. We can also talk about the result by adding *that* followed by a clause.

2 **Match the pictures and sentences.**

1 It was such a hot day that we went swimming.
2 I was so bored that I watched TV all day.
3 It was so hot that I burned my mouth.
4 I was feeling so energetic that I went for a swim.
5 I was so thirsty that I drank the whole glass at once.
6 It was such a scary movie that I couldn't watch.
7 The sun was so bright that I had to wear sunglasses.
8 I have such bad eyesight that I have to wear glasses.

3 **Circle the correct word.**

1 The movie was *such / so* long that I fell asleep.
2 I had *such / so* a bad dream that I couldn't get back to sleep.
3 The accident was *such / so* serious that they called a helicopter ambulance.
4 The lake was *such / so* dirty that we didn't go in it.
5 I have *such / so* a bad headache that I'm going to bed.
6 That's *such / so* a great idea, I just might do it.

4 **Rewrite the two sentences to make one single sentence. Use the word in parentheses.**

1 I was really hungry. I ordered another sandwich. (so)
I was so hungry that I ordered another sandwich.
2 The test was really difficult. I didn't pass it. (such) ....
3 The computer was very expensive. I couldn't afford it. (so) ....
4 The view was really beautiful. I had to take a photo. (such) ....
5 He speaks really fast. I don't understand a word he says. (so) ....
6 The game was really good. I didn't want it to end. (such) ....

Phrasal verbs

5 **Look at the dialogue on page 44 and complete the sentences below.**

Let's go and [1]........... .... at the mall.
Then they have an operation and [2]........... .... "Pretties."
They [3]........... .... and have parties all the time.
The government is after them before they [4]........... .... the truth.
If you start reading it, you'll really [5]........... .... it, I promise.
You'll have to [6]........... .... until I finish!

6 **Match the phrasal verbs in Exercise 5 with these definitions.**

1 become ....
2 discover ....
3 start to enjoy a lot ....
4 have fun ....
5 spend some time ....
6 wait ....

7 **The following contain verbs with prepositions. How are they different from phrasal verbs?**

There's this rebel group of kids who *run away* to escape the operation.
It's such a good book I can't *put* it *down*.

Many verbs in English are followed by prepositions. Sometimes this verb-preposition structure can't be immediately understood by looking at the individual words. These are called phrasal verbs.

8 **Circle the phrasal verbs in the sentences below. What do they mean?**

1 He really takes after his father. They like all the same things.
2 I'm sorry. I've just knocked over your glass of water.
3 Paul, stand up and come here.
4 Guess who I ran into today in town? Josh, I haven't seen him for years.
5 Can you turn up the volume? I can't hear a thing.
6 I've taken up judo. I'm not very good yet, but it's just the beginning.
7 I lent Max my bike and told him to take care of it.
8 The teacher told us not to play around.
9 I don't know how much it costs, but I'll look into it.
10 I ran after the bus, but I couldn't catch it.

9 **Complete the sentences with the phrasal verbs on this page.**

1 She really .... her mother.
2 It's a great game. You'll really .... it.
3 Kiss me and I'll .... a prince, I promise.
4 You'll have to .... for awhile. The firefighters are coming.
5 He's just .... yoga, so he's still got a lot to learn.
6 It was really nice to .... you. I haven't seen you for such a long time.

Skills

Reading

1 Read the book review. Does Brenda like the book?

++++

Hi, this is Brenda's Books online. This week the book I'm recommending is one I've been waiting to read for ages—and it's been well worth the wait. It is the latest spy adventure by Anthony Horowitz—*Crocodile Tears: An Alex Rider Novel.* I've been a big fan of Alex Rider, a teenage spy, ever since the first novel, *Stormbreaker.* This is the eighth book in the series and they just keep getting better.

For any of you who have never read an Alex Rider novel, Horowitz's hero is a kind of junior James Bond who works for MI6, but he's much cooler than James Bond and his missions are more dangerous. *Crocodile Tears* starts off with an explosion at a nuclear power station in India. The action then moves to Scotland where Alex is on vacation, to London, and then to Kenya. The book is full of action, and Alex faces a variety of dangerous situations as he deals with his latest adversary. But does he sort out his problems and save the world? Well, I know the answer because I've read the book but I'm not telling you. All I can promise is that you won't be disappointed. It's fast and exciting with action on every page. It's impossible to put down. I read it in two sittings and that's only because my mom insisted that I eat dinner with my family right in the middle of it.

Horowitz explains, "I think this has probably got more action in it than any other Alex Rider book so far. It's a little bit longer than normal and there are more action sequences."

2 Circle T (True) or F (False) for the sentences below.

1 Brenda was already a fan of the Alex Rider books. T / F
2 There have been four books between *Stormbreaker* and *Crocodile Tears.* T / F
3 Brenda thinks *Crocodile Tears* is the best of the Alex Rider books. T / F
4 Alex Rider works with James Bond. T / F
5 Alex is on vacation in Scotland. T / F
6 Brenda didn't finish the book in one sitting. T / F
7 Brenda thinks there's not enough action in the book. T / F

Listening

30 **3 Listen to Julie, Fred, and Farid talking about what they think of reading and about their favorite books. Answer the questions with their names.**

Who...

1 prefers TV to books?
2 loves reading
3 is reading a book about a movie?
4 likes horror stories?
5 reads two or three books every month?
6 likes fantasy stories
7 likes books for teenage girls?

Speaking and listening

4 **Read the beginning of the Alex Rider book *Snakehead*. Check the picture it describes.**

A 

B 

C 

Splash down.

Alex Rider would never forget the moment of impact, the first shock as the parachute opened and the second—more jolting still—as the module that had carried him back from outer space crashed into the sea. Was it his imagination or was there steam rising up all around him? Maybe it was sea spray. It didn't matter. He was back. That was all he cared about. He had made it. He was still alive.

He was lying on his back, crammed into the tiny capsule with his knees tucked into his chest. Half closing his eyes, Alex experienced a moment of extraordinary stillness. He was motionless. His fists were clenched. He wasn't breathing. Already he found it impossible to believe that the events that had led to his journey into space had really taken place. He tried to imagine himself hurtling around the earth at seventeen and a half thousand miles an hour. It couldn't have happened. It had surely all been part of some incredible dream.

5 **Find these words in the text and circle the best definition for each one.**

1 jolting
   a) moving in a sudden, strong way b) quiet c) in a relaxed way
2 module
   a) a parachute b) part of a spaceship c) a small boat
3 crammed
   a) with not much room b) with a lot of room c) asleep
4 clenched fist
   a) 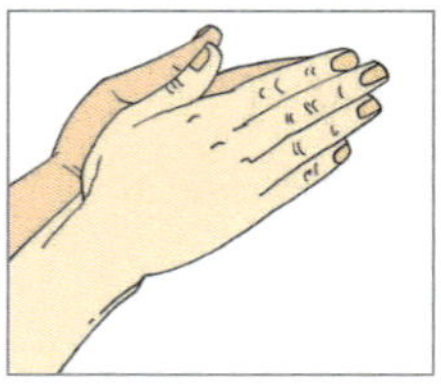 b) 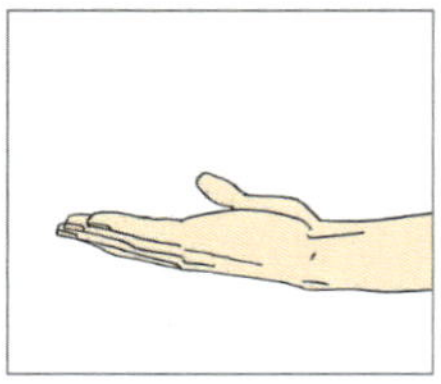 c) 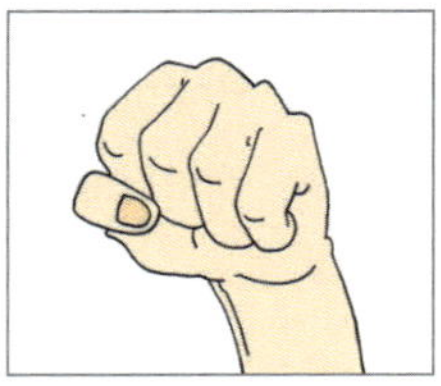
5 hurtling
   a) moving slowly b) moving quickly c) moving really quickly

6 ***"Already he found it impossible to believe that the events that had led to his journey into space had really taken place."***
Work with a partner. Decide what those events may have been. Make up a short story. Tell your story to the rest of the class and vote on the best one.

Speaking and writing

7 **Think of the last book you read and write notes to answer the questions.**

- *Title / author?*
- *What kind of book is it?*
- *What's it about?*
- *Did you like it? Why/why not?*

8 **Work with a partner. Ask and answer questions about your books.**

9 **Read the review below and answer the questions.**

1 What happens in the book?
2 Did Anahita like it? (Why/why not?)

- *Book: Dead Girls Don't Write Letters*
- *Author: Gail Giles*
- *What's it about?*

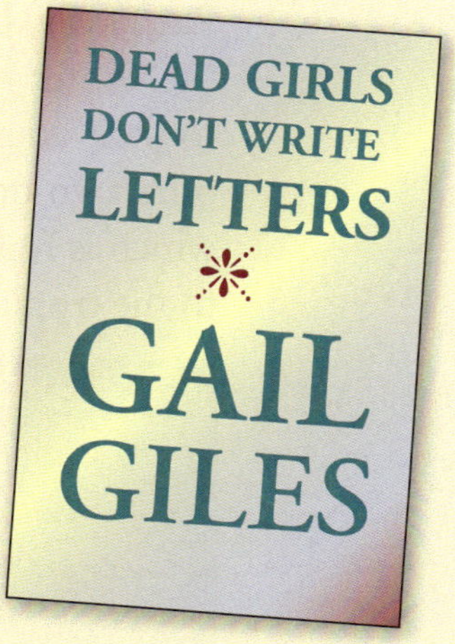

Sunny's sister Jazz (who is NOT a nice girl) dies in a fire. Her parents are really sad, but one day Sunny gets a letter from Jazz. "I'll be coming home soon," it says. And in fact, one day Jazz turns up. She has turned into a nice, friendly girl, and she knows everything about the family's past. But Sunny asks herself a big question: Who is this stranger who says she's Jazz? She knows that dead girls can't write letters!

- *What do I think of it?*

Wow! This is really a good book. It's so exciting and full of twists. I liked the idea that the sisters are so different (aren't they often in real life?) and that suddenly the bad one is good. What do you do if you've always been the good one? I won't tell you the ending, but I can tell you that there are a couple of surprises. And have a look at Giles' next book. It's called Playing in Traffic, and it's a thriller, too.
(Review by Anahita)

10 **Expand your notes from Exercise 7 and write a book report. Use the model above to help you.**

Sounds right Stress in compound nouns

31 **11** **In compound words, the stress is normally on the first syllable in the word. Underline the syllable that is stressed in the words below. Then listen and check.**

comic book   horror story   poetry book   science fiction

Migration

Key words

migrate	breeding grounds	current	Arctic tern
migratory animals/birds	predators	salmon	ruby-throated
breed	supply	blue whale	hummingbird

1 Read the article and match the headings to the paragraphs.

1 24-hour sunlight
2 North and south
3 The final journey
4 Size isn't important
5 Flying through water

A ☐

Each year, blue whales travel thousands of kilometers in search of food. They spend the winter months in the warm waters of the tropics where many of them give birth to their young. When summer arrives, some of them migrate south to Antarctica, and others go north to the Arctic. All of them are looking for the rich supply of plankton which is found in polar waters. After three or four months of feeding, they swim back to the tropics.

B ☐

Pacific salmon are famous for their difficult journeys of hundreds of kilometers from the ocean to their breeding grounds up American rivers. When they start the journey, their bodies are very strong, but as soon as the salmon leave the ocean, they stop eating.

They swim upriver, fighting against strong currents and jumping up waterfalls. Many are eaten by predators or caught by fishermen. Months later, the lucky ones arrive, but they are exhausted. They have just enough energy to lay their eggs before they die.

C ☐

Arctic terns fly an incredible 40,000 km every year as they travel between the North and South poles. They also probably see more daylight than any other animal on Earth. In their northern home during the summer, the sun doesn't set, and they experience the same long days in their winter home in Antarctica.

D ☐

They may only weigh a couple of grams, but when it comes to long-distance flying, ruby-throated hummingbirds are big birds. Twice a year, these amazing creatures take off from the U.S. on a 2,400-km journey before they finally land in Costa Rica. This journey includes a 960-km, 20-hour nonstop flight across the Gulf of Mexico.

E ☐

They can't fly but that doesn't stop penguins from getting around. They are the only birds that migrate by swimming. Using currents, they can migrate from Antarctica as far up the east coast of South America as Rio de Janeiro in Brazil.

Mini-project Research on migratory birds

2 **Choose one of these birds.**

stork   wild goose   starling   crane   puffin

Search the Internet or a library for information about their migration. Think about the questions below. Write a short paragraph to answer each question.

Where do they live?
Where do they migrate to?
Why do they migrate?
How far do they travel?
What dangers are there on their journey?

Biology

UNIT 6 The main event

32 1 **Listen and read.**

In this unit

You learn
- the passive
- *make / let / be allowed to*
- words for special events

and then you can
- talk about ambition
- say where things are done
- say what people let you do

Tennis anyone?

From the U.S. Open to Wimbledon, kids around the world work hard to make tennis tournaments come alive.

My name is Sheri and I'm a huge tennis fan. I always wanted to experience a Grand Slam tournament. Every year, there are four Grand Slam events—the Australian Open, the French Open, the U.S. Open, and Wimbledon. And last year I got to go to one of them and watch the best tennis players in the world play—for free. How? I became a ball girl at the U.S. Open!

Each year about 270 ball girls and boys are chosen to work at the U.S. Open. Many ball boys and girls come back year after year, but some teenagers try out for the role, too.

Last year, 300 of us tried out for 70 ball-person positions. The tryouts lasted for two exhausting months. "What?" I can hear you thinking, "Two-month-long tryouts? What's so difficult about picking up tennis balls?" Sorry, but you really have no idea! When we first applied, they made us run for 12 minutes, and then stand completely still for four minutes! Does that sound easy? Try it sometime!

Being a ball boy or girl can be dangerous, too. A few years ago at Wimbledon, for example, a ball boy was hit by a 200 kph serve from Pete Sampras, the champion at the time, but the ball boy just smiled and kept going!

Anyway, in the end I was selected, so I went to the U.S. Open and did my stuff. It was great! It was so exciting to be so close to some of my favorite players. I couldn't talk to them since ball boys and girls aren't allowed to talk to players during the matches. But after the matches ended, players would let us take photographs and ask for autographs.

I wasn't paid any money and I had to work hard, but I had an amazing two weeks. I am hoping that I can go back and be a ball girl again for at least a couple more years!

2 **Circle T (True) or F (False) for the sentences below.**

1 Sheri is a huge football fan. T / F
2 She trained for five months to be a ball girl. T / F
3 Being a ball boy or girl isn't easy. T / F
4 A ball boy went to the hospital when a ball hit him. T / F
5 Sheri talked to some players during the matches. T / F
6 She doesn't want to be a ball girl again this year. T / F

Get talking Talking about permission

33 **3** **Match the questions and answers. Then listen and check.**

1 Why don't you wear a hat to school?
2 Why weren't you at the party?
3 Why don't you take your cell phone to school?
4 Why isn't there a TV in your bedroom?

a) I wasn't allowed to go.
b) We're not allowed to use them there.
c) I'm not allowed to have one.
d) We're not allowed to wear them.

4 **Work with a partner. Use the prompts to make short conversations.**

A Are you allowed to .... ?

B Yes, but I'm not allowed to ....

✓ go to parties
✗ come home late

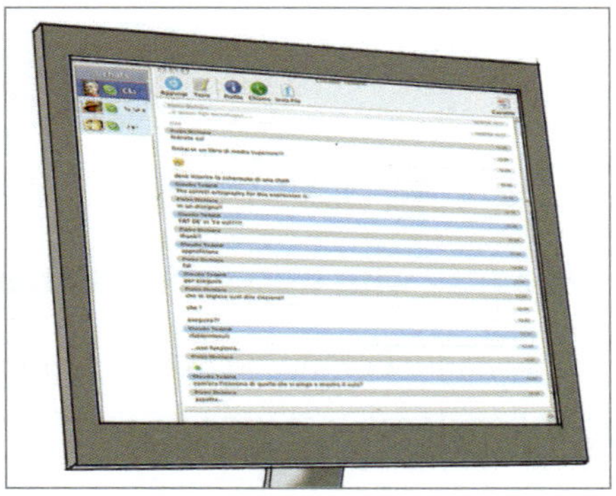

✓ surf the Internet
✗ go into chat rooms

✓ buy your own clothes
✗ dye my hair

✓ invite friends over
✗ make a lot of noise

✓ go to fast-food restaurants
✗ eat fast-food every day

Language Focus

Vocabulary Special events

1 Match the words and pictures.

- [ ] car show
- [ ] school fair
- [ ] fashion show
- [ ] music festival
- [ ] tennis tournament
- [ ] movie premiere
- [ ] bike race
- [ ] book fair

2 Where would you expect to find these people?

actors	fans	teachers	models
athletes	authors	rock stars	journalists

Get talking Talking about events

34 **3 Complete the dialogues with the replies. Listen and check.**

1 I saw some really cool clothing designs and hair styles.
2 Yes, I went to Lollapalooza last year.
3 Yes, there was one at the mall last year.
4 It was fantastic. All my favorite bands were there.

A Have you ever been to a rock festival?
B 1 Yes, I went to Lollapalooza last year.
A What was it like?
B 2 ....

A Have you ever been to a fashion show?
B 3 ....
A What was it like?
B 4 ....

4 Work with a partner. Ask each other questions about the events in Exercise 1. Use the dialogues from Exercise 3 to help you.

Grammar

The passive

1 **Complete the sentences from the texts on page 54 with the words on the right.**

was hit
are chosen
aren't allowed
wasn't paid

1 Each year ball boys and girls ....
2 A ball boy .... by a 200 kph serve.
3 Ball boys and girls .... to talk to the players.
4 I .... any money.

The simple present passive has the following structure:
Subject + simple present of **be (not) + past participle**.

2 **Read the sentences. Which events from Exercise 1 on page 56 are they talking about?**

1 The movie is shown to a specially invited audience.
2 The cars are washed every morning.
3 The parents of the children are all invited.
4 The race leader wears a yellow shirt.
5 The champion wins $500,000.
6 Bands from all over the U.S. come to play.

3 **Complete the sentences with the simple present passive form of the verb.**

How it works: A rock festival

1 First a big field .... (find) for the event.
2 Then the bands .... (choose) and .... (invite) to play.
3 The festival .... (advertise) on the radio and in newspapers.
4 Tickets .... (sold) on the Internet.
5 A big stage .... (build) in the field.
6 Security .... (arrange).
7 The gates .... (open)
8 Finally the fans .... (search) when they arrive.

The simple past passive has the following structure:
Subject + simple past of **be (not) + past participle**.

4 **Rewrite the underlined sentences. Use the past passive.**

1 The school fashion show was a great success. [1] They invited 100 people and most of them came. [2] They raised more than $1,000 for charity. It really was a big event and there were even a few local celebrities there. [3] The photographers took tons of pictures and [4] the newspaper put the show on its front page. The clothes were great. [5] Teenagers designed them all. It was amazing. In fact, [6] the teenagers planned the whole evening. [7] A 16-year-old boy wrote the music and [8] a 14-year-old girl did the lights. It was amazing to see what a group of teenagers can do.

1 100 people were invited.
2 More than $1,000 ....
3 Tons of pictures ....
4 The show ....
5 All the clothes ....
6 ....
7 ....
8 ....

Make / let / be allowed to

5 **Complete the sentences from the text on page 54. Use *made / let / allowed.***

1 They .... us run for 12 minutes.
2 Ball boys and girls aren't .... to talk to players during the matches.
3 Players would .... us take photographs.

> **Note**
> The past tense of ***let*** is ***let***

6 **Nick is at a camp. Write sentences starting with *They make him / don't make him / let him / don't let him...***

1 make / get up / six o'clock every morning
They make him get up at six o'clock every morning.
2 not let / stay up later than 10:00 p.m.
3 make / help serve the food
4 not make / help with the cleaning
5 let / watch football on TV
6 make / put up his own tent
7 not let / stay in the tent during the day
8 let / use the Internet in the camp office

7 **Match the signs and the sentences.**

1 You aren't allowed to keep the lights on after 11:00 p.m.
2 Dogs aren't allowed.
3 You aren't allowed to walk on the grass.
4 You aren't allowed to feed the animals.
5 You aren't allowed to run.
6 You aren't allowed to use cell phones.

8 **Write sentences using the correct form of *be allowed to.***

1 James ✓ watch TV / ✗ not watch TV after 10 o'clock.
James is allowed to watch TV, but he isn't allowed to watch TV after 10 o'clock.
2 Sarah ✓ go to bed late / ✗ not get up late
....
3 We ✓ wear jeans to school / ✗ not wear shorts
....
4 They ✓ listen to music / ✗ not listen without headphones
....
5 I ✓ go to my friend's house / ✗ not stay overnight
....
6 She ✓ have parties at home / ✗ not play loud music
....

Skills

Reading

1 **Read the magazine article. Find out what these numbers refer to.**

a) more than 3 million b) 200,000 c) between 1 and 2 million d) 5,000

Really big events? Rio's the place!

Soccer crowds

The largest number of people ever at a soccer game was in 1950 at the final of the Soccer World Cup at the Maracanã Stadium in Rio de Janeiro. The stadium was built for the World Cup, and everyone in Brazil was sure that Brazil would win. They went to see the final against Uruguay, and only needed a tie to be the champions. A total of 173,850 people paid to go in and watch, but journalists and officials made the number 200,000 or so. But, to the disappointment of the Brazilians, Uruguay won 2-1 to take the World Cup for the second time.

Rock concerts

There have been some enormous rock concerts in Rio. In 1994, Rod Stewart played on the beach in Copacabana on December 31, and it is estimated that more than 3 million people were there—a world record. The Rolling Stones played on the beach just before Rio Carnival in 2006, but they only(!) got about 1.2 million people to come and watch. And there have been three "Rock in Rio" festivals, with hundreds of thousand of fans going over three or four days to watch bands such as R.E.M. and Red Hot Chili Peppers.

Carnival

The number of people at Rio Carnival is difficult to measure, at least if you're thinking about the number of people in the streets of Rio. But one thing is for sure: the parade of samba schools in the Sambódromo is huge. Each year, during two consecutive nights, the 14 top samba schools in Rio parade through the stadium. Each school has between 4,000 and 5,000 people, and each school takes 80 minutes to parade. The special stadium, which was built in 1984, holds 65,000 people, but millions of people watch on TV, too.

New Year's Eve

New Year's Eve is a big event almost everywhere in the world, but there are very few places where it's bigger than Copacabana in Rio de Janeiro. Usually there are between 1 and 2 million people on the beach to watch the fireworks that begin at midnight. These days, after the fireworks there are usually two or three simultaneous concerts on the beach with famous musicians. The party goes on, of course, into the daylight hours!

2 **Read the text again. Answer the questions.**

1 Why was the Maracanã Stadium built?
2 Why were the Brazilians disappointed in 1950?
3 Who takes part in the parades in the Sambódromo each year?
4 How many people can watch the samba school parade in the Sambódromo?
5 How long do "Rock in Rio" festivals last?
6 What time does the New Year's Eve party finish?

Listening

3 **Say the numbers in the table.**

20	312,000	687	42,000
140,000	500,000	27,000	2 billion

35 **Where do you think the numbers go in the text below? Fill in the blanks, and then listen and check.**

Total number of spectators: [1]........................ (40,000 people a day)
Amount of strawberries: [2]........................ kilograms
Number of bottles of water: [3]......................
Number of ice creams: [4]........................
Number of matches: [5]....................
Number of courts: [6]......................
Number of tennis balls: [7]........................
Number of TV viewers: [8]......................

THE CHAMPIONSHIPS WIMBLEDON

Speaking and listening

36 **4** **Listen to a group of students discussing the task on the right. Make a note of their answers to the questions.**

5 **Work in small groups and plan your own event. Present your ideas to the class.**

Task: You are going to plan an event to raise money for charity.

1 What kind of event are you going to choose?
2 What things do you need to plan?
3 Who is going to do what?
4 How much money do you want to make?
5 What kind of charity are you going to give it to?

Writing

6 **Look at Sally's poster for the rock festival. Write a similar poster for your own event.**

11A productions proudly present
King High School Experience
Rock Festival
Featuring:
The Flying Pigs,
Overdrive,
Skool Rulez, and The Henriettas.
When: Saturday July 1
Where: School football field
Tickets only $5 for the whole day
See **Leroy Sparks** (11A)
Let us entertain you!

Check your progress Units 5 and 6

1 Complete the words.

1 c_ _ _ _ _ _ _ _ _ _ of short stories
2 rock f_ _ _ _ _ _ _
3 detective n_ _ _ _
4 fashion s_ _ _
5 school f_ _ _
6 tennis t_ _ _ _ _ _ _ _ _
7 nonf_ _ _ _ _ _ book
8 movie pre_ _ _ _

8

2 Complete the sentences.

1 It's a comedy, it's _ _ _ _ _ .
2 It's a sci-fi, it's _ _ _ _ _ _ _ _ _ .
3 It's a _ _ _ _ _ _ _ _ _ _ , it's interesting.
4 It's a horror story, it's _ _ _ _ _ .
5 It's a _ _ _ _ _ _ _ _ _ , it's thrilling.

5

3 Complete the dialogues. Use the passive (present or past) and *so/such.*

1 A This is [1].............. a good book.
B Who [2].............. it .... (write) by?
A Philip Pullman. It's great. I'm [3].............. excited about what happens next.
B I think that book [4].............. (chose) for a prize.
A Yes, it was. He's [5].............. a good writer!

2 A There's a music festival on the weekend. It [6]....................... (advertise) in the local newspaper. There are [7]....................... a lot of famous groups coming!
B It's [8]....................... wet though. It might not happen.
A Don't say that! I've already got a ticket! The tickets [9]....................... (sell) online.
B Were they? I'm [10]....................... terrible with computers! I never buy anything online.
A It's not [11]....................... a difficult thing to do! Come on! I'll help you!

11

4 Complete using *so* or *such*.

1 That was .... silly of you.
2 Gina was .... tired that she went straight to bed.
3 This is .... an interesting book!
4 I have never seen .... a bad movie!
5 He's going to buy me a book. That's .... a great idea!

5

5 Complete the phrasal verbs.

1 I .... into your sister at the mall.
2 Oh wow! I love this song! .... it up!
3 Jim's .... up horseback riding. He'd never tried it before!
4 Who do you .... after most, your mom or your dad?
5 Billy .... over a glass of water onto my cell phone!
6 Sometimes I need to read half a book before I .... into it.

6

6 Rewrite the sentences using the passive.

1 They chose our school to enter the contest.
....
2 They always invite parents to the school fair.
....
3 A falling light hit a fan at the concert.
....
4 They searched the girl.
....
5 We plan a party at the end of every year.
....

10

7 Complete using *make, let,* or *be allowed.*

1 My teachers .... me do too much work.
2 I .... to go out tonight. My mom said no.
3 They won't .... me watch that movie.
4 She .... me try her new shoes.
5 He .... me to drive his car.

5

TOTAL 50

My progress so far is ...

great! ☐ good. ☐ poor. ☐

Marathons!

1 Read the text and decide if the sentences below are T (True) or F (False).

1 There are some difficult hills in the San Francisco Marathon. T / F
2 The St. George Marathon is shorter than most. T / F
3 Anyone can sign up to run in the Boston Marathon. T / F
4 There is a marathon where you run on ice. T / F
5 In the marathon in the Himalayas, you have to run up Mt. Everest. T / F

Marathons are run everywhere. There are a lot to choose from if you want to see different places. In just about every major city and even in remote places. Perhaps the best-known is the Boston Marathon. It has been taking place for more than 100 years. Runners need to qualify for Boston, so only the best runners participate in this race. Other popular marathons include the scenic (and largely downhill) St. George Marathon in Utah, the Chicago Marathon, and the San Francisco Marathon, which has a few tough hills! There's also the New York City Marathon. With its 39,000 participants, you'd have no shortage of company. For people who want to travel farther, marathons are also held in the North Pole, where you run on ice! There's even a marathon in the Himalayas, but you don't have to run up Mt. Everest!

37 **2 Listen and try to match the people in the New York City Marathon to the charities they supported. Then listen again and check.**

Competitor	Charity
Dressed in red tank tops	Maasai Warriors
In yellow jerseys	Fred's Team
As themselves	Team for Kids

Do you know?

Originally, there was no fixed distance for the marathon race. 40 kilometers became the standard until the 1908 Olympic Games in London, when the race was made longer so that members of the royal family could see the start and finish. We use that same distance today—42.195 kilometers.

38 **3 Look at the table below and try to complete the missing times. Then listen and check your answers.**

Competitor	Time
Fastest man	1..... hours 2..... minutes 14 seconds
Fastest woman	3..... hours 4..... minutes 25 seconds

4 Over 2 U! Imagine you are going to take part in a marathon. In groups, decide which charity you'd like to raise money for and design a costume to wear. Find out about that charity. Write a paragraph about it and present it to the class.

American MORE! Now you can watch Episode 3 of *School Reporters*! DVD

Chill out at Lollapalooza

Want some ideas for things to do in the summer? Here's my highlight from last August. I went to Lollapalooza for three days with my older brother Daniel.
What's Lollapalooza? A three-day music festival with eight separate stages and tons of bands. It started on a Friday and lasted for three days. Great bands! I liked The Killers, Jane's Addiction, Kings of Leon, and Vampire Weekend best. It was awesome.
Daniel's been going to Lollapalooza for a couple of years now. He says he's had some great experiences there. Here's an example. The first time Cage the Elephant came to Lollapalooza, they played in a tent with about 1,000 people in it, all standing up. When they'd been playing for some time, people started crowdsurfing. I could never do it, but Daniel launched himself up and was carried along by the crowd. Daniel says it was scary, but like nothing else he'd experienced ever before.
We stayed at an apartment where one of Daniel's friends lives. There were about 12 of us staying there. But all we did was go there to sleep. The next morning we were up to see more music.
Four more things I liked about the weekend:
Number 1. There was a big section of really cool eco-vendors.
Number 2. Grant Park, where the festival's held, is a really cool place in downtown Chicago.
Number 3. There was an autograph booth where you can meet your favorite bands.
Number 4. Last but not least, the toilets were clean (and believe me, at a music festival, that's important!)

So if you want something a little different to do this year, you could try Lollapalooza. Just check out www.lollapalooza.com.

For MORE! Go to www.more-online.com/american and take a quiz on this text.

Herbert Puchta & Jeff Stranks
G. Gerngross C. Holzmann P. Lewis-Jones

American MORE! 4A

COMBO Workbook

HELBLING LANGUAGES
CAMBRIDGE UNIVERSITY PRESS
editora ática

CONTENTS

UNIT 1 Football? Soccer?

2 **1 Complete the dialogue using the words below. Then listen and check.**

been bought doing for lived looking see since visiting wanted

Jess Hi, Emma!

Emma Hi! Sorry I'm late. Wow, what are all these people [1]........................ here today?

Jess The football stadium isn't far from here. There must be a game today. It's funny, I've [2]........................ here [3]........................ I was born, but I've never been to the stadium before. Have you ever been to a football game?

Emma Yes, I've [4]........................ to a few games—high-school games! Hey, do you [5]........................ that cute guy over there? I think he's lost ... Hello! Are you [6]........................ for the stadium?

Zach Oh, hi. Yes, I am!

Jess It's not far from here. Just walk straight ahead and then turn right at the end of the street. Where are you from?

Zach I'm from Colorado. I'm just [7]........................ .

Emma How long have you been here?

Zach [8]........................ a week. I've always [9]........................ to see a professional football game ... Have you [10]........................ tickets, too?

Jess No, we aren't going to the game. We're going to have lunch! Do you want to join us before the game starts? There's a good place to eat close to the stadium.

Zach OK! That sounds great!

2 Answer the questions.

1 Why does Emma say she's sorry?
2 Why are there so many people around?
3 How long has Jess lived in the area?
4 Where does Zach live?
5 Why is he in town?

Talking on the phone

3 **3 Listen to two dialogues. Match the speaker and the activity.**

1 Max — a) doing homework
2 Kelly — b) shopping
3 Eve — c) traveling somewhere

4 **4 Listen again and answer the questions.**

1 What is Kelly thinking of buying?
2 Who is Max meeting?
3 What is he doing this weekend?
4 Where is Eve?

Language Focus

Vocabulary Sports apparel

1 **List the items that each person is wearing. Then write the correct letter next to each sport.**

cleats	glove	goggles	helmet	pads
shirt	shorts	socks	sneakers	tank top

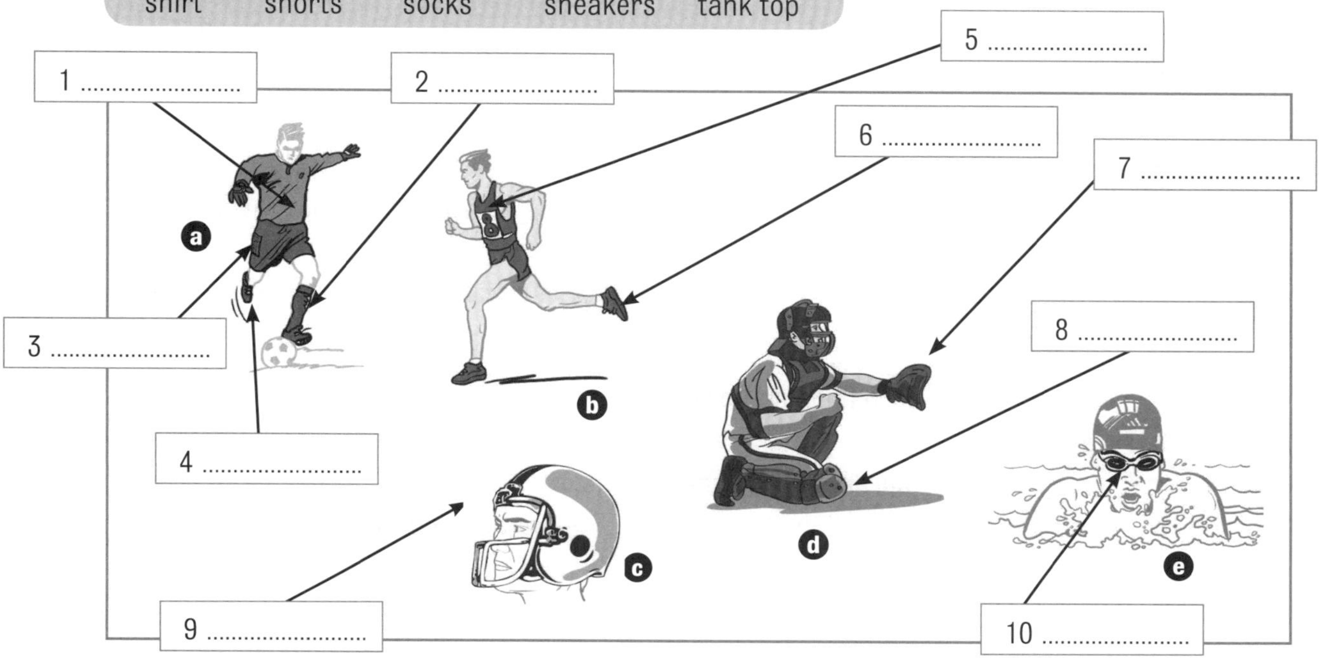

football .... swimming .... running .... soccer .... baseball ....

2 **Which words from Exercise 1 can be used with *a pair of* ...? Write them below.**

1 ....
2 ....
3 ....
4 ....
5 ....
6 ....
7 ....

Buying things in a sporting goods store

5 **3** **Complete the dialogue using the words below. Then listen and check.**

help	pair	size	try

Salesclerk Can I [1]............................. you?
Customer Yes, I need a [2]............................. of bike shorts.
Salesclerk OK. What [3]............................. are you?
Customer About a 10, I think.
Salesclerk OK, why don't you [4]............................. these on?
Customer Thanks.

Grammar

Simple present / present continuous / present perfect (review)

1 Write the number of the sentences in the correct place in the table.

Habits, routines	Things happening now	Experiences someone has had up to now
2		

1 Have you ever been to Egypt?
~~2 What time do you get up?~~
3 What are you listening to?
4 Are you surfing the Internet?
5 Where do they play baseball?
6 What's the best movie you've ever seen?
7 What have you done to your hair?
8 Who are you talking to?
9 Are you scared of heights?
10 What are you studying in science this semester?

2 Complete the sentences with the present perfect of the verbs in parentheses.

1 What's that nice smell? .... fresh bread? (you make)
2 I .... to learn Spanish. (always want)
3 I'm sure I know you. .... somewhere before? (we meet)
4 .... your library books back? (you take)
5 I'm not ready to run a marathon. I .... enough. (not train)
6 How long .... the same hairdo? (you have)
7 We .... a test for about two months. (not have)
8 Maybe that letter will arrive later today. The mail .... (not come) yet.

3 Circle the correct verb.

1 **A** Sarah! Can you pick up the phone? It's someone for you.
  B I can't come now. *I wash/I'm washing* my hair!
2 **A** Why aren't you eating your hamburger?
  B It's disgusting. *I'm not liking/I don't like* it.
3 **A** Can I borrow your phone for a minute?
  B Not right now. *I wait/I'm waiting* for an important call.
4 **A** Have you finished that book?
  B No, *I still read/I'm still reading* it.
5 **A** Where's Alan?
  B I don't know. *I'm not seeing/I haven't seen* him for a long time.
6 **A** You know this town really well, don't you?
  B Of course! *I've lived/I lived* here since I was born!

4 Read the email and answer the questions.

Hi Kate

How are you doing with your studying? I've just been studying for math, and I'm working on history now. French isn't a problem for me since I practice a few words and grammar structures every day.

Talk to you later.

Jan

1 What has Jan already studied? ....
2 What does she practice every day? ....
3 What is she studying right now? ....

5 Complete the questions and short answers.

1 Have Mike and Jenny *arrived*? (arrive) No, they ....
2 .... you .... your homework? (do) Yes, I ....
3 .... he .... the new U2 CD? (buy) Yes, he ....
4 .... your parents .... on vacation? (go) No, they ....

6 Complete each sentence with the correct tense of the verb in parentheses.

1 Hurry up! You .... on the phone since 10 o'clock! (be)
2 I .... usually .... *Lost* on TV. (not watch)
But this series .... really good during the past few weeks. (be)
3 James .... to karate lessons twice a week. (go)
4 I can't find my purse anywhere. Are you sure you .... it? (not see)
5 .... you .... any good books right now? (read)
6 I .... often .... crossword puzzles. (not do)
7 Shh! I .... to a really interesting talk show. (listen)

7 Match the questions and answers.

1 Have you ever ridden on a motorcycle?
2 Do you ever go mountain biking?
3 How long have you had that watch?
4 Has your hair always been blonde?
5 Have you finished the crossword puzzle?
6 What's the most exciting thing you've ever done?
7 Have you ever eaten deer?

a) For about four years.
b) I went snowboarding last year.
c) No, but I've done most of it.
d) No, I haven't. I'm a vegetarian!
e) No, I don't.
f) Yes, I have.
g) Yes, since I was born.

Skills

Listening

1 **Look at the photo and the advertisement for a TV documentary and guess the answers to the questions.**

1 Where and what do free-climbers climb?
  a) cliffs along the coast
  b) buildings in cities
  c) rocks in the country

2 What do they use to climb?
  a) ropes
  b) ladders
  c) bare hands

3 Why is Alain Robert called the human spider?
  a) He wears a Spiderman costume when he climbs.
  b) He uses ropes that make him look like a spider.
  c) He climbs vertically just like a spider.

4 How many climbs has he done?
  a) 10
  b) More than 50
  c) 50

6 **2** **Listen and check your answers.**

Reading

3 **Read the article and answer the questions.**

Would you enjoy clinging to the vertical wall on the outside of a 90-floor office block with hundreds of people watching you from the ground—and police waiting to arrest you when you reached the top of the building?
Well, it's just a normal day in the life of Alain Robert, "the human spider."
Alain is a world-famous French "free urban climber." Free-climbers like Alain don't usually use any ropes, helmets, or other safety equipment. They climb using just their bare hands and climbing shoes. It's one of the most dangerous extreme sports in the world. And Alain doesn't climb for fame or money, although he has earned money through climbing some buildings for advertising. For example, in 2003 he climbed a building in London, England, wearing a Spiderman costume, to promote the movie.
He began climbing rock cliffs as a young boy. His first "free climb" was when he was around 12. He'd forgotten his keys and couldn't get into his home on the seventh floor of an apartment building. So instead of waiting for his parents to come home, he climbed up the outside of the building and got in through an open window. He says

that from that moment on, he wanted to be a climber.
Since then, he has climbed more than 80 of the world's tallest buildings, often without permission. He has been arrested several times after these climbs, and has had five serious falls in his life. But none of these experiences has stopped him from attempting more and more dangerous climbs.
He admits that he puts his life in danger every time he climbs, but he says that climbing this way has now become "a habit." Which building is he planning to climb next? We'll have to wait and see!

1 How long has Alain Robert been free-climbing?
2 How many buildings has he climbed?
3 Has anyone ever paid him for climbing? When? Why?
4 Has he ever had serious accidents?
5 Why do the police often arrest him after his climbs?
6 Which building is he planning to climb next?

Writing for your Portfolio

4 **Read the questions in Exercises 1 and 3 again. Write an imaginary interview with Alain Robert using the information from the article.**

Paragraph 1: Explain who Alain Robert is and why he is famous.
Paragraph 2: Write your questions and his answers.
Paragraph 3: Say what you think about Alain Robert and free-climbing.

UNIT 2 Space and beyond

7 **1 Complete the dialogue using the words below. Then listen and check.**

bored excited happy hungry nervous sad

1 **Kathy** What's up with the big smile, Nick?
Nick I've had some good news! Remember that competition I entered? Well, I've won!
Kathy No wonder you look so [1]........................ Congratulations!

2 **Kathy** I'm [2]........................ . There's nobody around to do anything with.
Mom Why don't you call Laura?
Kathy I called her this morning, but she'd already gone out.

3 **Nick** Shall we go get something to eat before the game?
Luke No, I had dinner before I left. I'm not very [3]........................ .

4 **Kathy** Are you feeling [4]........................ about the history final, too?
Luke Yes. And what's worse, I couldn't study the last unit. I lost my notes.
Kathy Why didn't you ask me to lend you mine?
Luke I called you last night, but you were already in bed!

5 **Nick** What's wrong, Kathy? You look so [5]........................ .
Kathy It's my grandfather. He cut himself badly while he was working in his yard yesterday. By the time he got to the hospital, he'd already lost a lot of blood. He's still in the hospital now.
Nick Oh, I'm so sorry to hear that. I hope he gets better soon.

6 **Luke** You must be really [6]........................ about going to Japan.
Kathy Yes, I can't wait! I've never been before, but I've heard it's amazing.

2 Answer the questions.

1 What did Nick find out about the competition he'd entered? ....
2 Why couldn't Kathy speak to Laura on the phone? ....
3 Who had already eaten, Nick or Luke? ....
4 Why wasn't Luke able to borrow Kathy's notes? ....
5 What was Kathy's grandfather doing before he had the accident? ....
6 Why was Kathy looking forward to going to Japan? ....

Giving reasons

3 Match the questions and answers.

1 Why are you so bored?
2 You look happy! What's happened?
3 You're jumping up and down! Why are you so excited?
4 Why aren't you hungry?
5 Why are you nervous?
6 Why do you look so sad?

a) Because I failed my music exam.
b) I just heard some amazing news!
c) Because I have to give a presentation in front of the whole school, in English!
d) Because we're winning the game! Look at the score!
e) Because I finished my book and I have nothing to do.
f) Because I had so much to eat at lunchtime.

Language Focus

Vocabulary Travel

1 Match the pictures and captions. Then number the pictures in the correct order.

The plane takes off. ....
He gets to the airport. ....
Dave sets out on his trip. ....
The plane lands. ....
He gets on the plane. ....
He gets into the taxi. ....
He gets off the plane. ....
The flight takes four hours. ....

8 **2 Listen to the dialogue and answer the questions.**

1 What time did they set out? ....
2 What time did they get to the train station? ....
3 Why couldn't they get on the train right away? ....
4 How long did it take to get to Baltimore? ....
5 What time did they get off the train? ....

Talking about your trip to school

9 **3 Complete the dialogue. Use the prepositions below. Then listen and check.**

at off out on to (x 3) up

Tom How do you get [1]............................ school every day?
Claire I walk [2]............................ the bus stop, then I get [3]............................ the school bus.
Tom So what time do you set [4]............................ in the morning?
Claire I get [5]............................ around seven, and I get [6]............................ the bus stop at about a quarter past eight.
Tom Does the bus stop right outside school?
Claire Yes, I get [7]............................ the bus at the main entrance to my school.
Tom What time do you arrive [8]............................ school?
Claire By about quarter to nine.

Grammar

Past continuous vs. simple past

1 Write sentences. Use the simple past and past continuous tenses.

Example:

2:30 Tony / talk / on his phone
2:32 the battery / go dead

Tony was talking on his phone when the battery went dead.

1 10:00 Gabriella / walk down the street
10:10 she / trip

....

2 11:00 We / do an exercise
11:05 the bell / ring

....

3 11:30 My parents / watch / TV
11:40 they / hear / a knock at the door

....

4 7:30 My sister / brush / her teeth
7:32 her tooth / fall out

....

5 8:15 We / eat / dinner
8:17 the lights / go out

....

2 Circle the action that happened first in each sentence.

1 I'd only had my skateboard for a week before it broke.
2 They scored when they'd only been playing for 10 minutes.
3 When I arrived, you'd already left.
4 Jane didn't come to the movie theater. She'd seen the movie.
5 Lily was washing her hair when the phone rang downstairs.
6 Who were you talking to when I saw you yesterday?
7 We'd driven for half an hour when we realized we were lost.
8 I'd known Jerry for two years when he came to our school.

3 Read the sentences and answer the questions.

1 a) While I waited for the train, I wrote some emails.
b) While I waited for the train, I was writing some emails.
Which speaker finished the emails, a or b? ....

2 a) When we got there, Patrick was fixing dinner.
b) When we got there, Patrick fixed dinner.
Which speaker smelled food when she arrived, a or b? ....

3 a) The teacher was scolding me when I laughed out loud.
b) The teacher scolded me when I laughed out loud.
Which speaker got into trouble for laughing, a or b? ....

Past perfect

4 Complete the sentences with the past perfect form of the verbs in parentheses.

1 **A** Why was the teacher angry with Ivan?
B Because he .... his homework for the second time last week. (not do)
2 I was just getting on the bus when I realized I .... my ticket. (forget)
3 When I got home, the rain .... (stop)
4 Suddenly I remembered where I .... her before. (meet)
5 I was disappointed to learn that I .... the test. (not pass)
6 The river bed was completely dry. It .... for a long time. (not rain)

Narrative tenses (review)

5 Complete the story with the past continuous, simple past, or past perfect form of the verbs in parentheses.

Three-year-old throws away family's money

A three-year-old girl [1]........................... (throw) all the money a Chinese couple [2]........................... (save) for several months out of the window of their apartment while her parents [3]........................... (sleep).
"When I woke up, my purse was on the bed. It was open, but all the money inside it [4]........................... (disappear)," said the mother.
"I immediately asked my daughter what [5]........................... (happen), but she said she [6]........................... (not know). I looked everywhere! When I saw a couple of bills on the windowsill, I realized what she [7]........................... (do)."
The owner of a restaurant below the apartment said he saw the money as it came flying down from the sky. "People in the street [8]........................... (go) crazy trying to catch it," he explained.
The couple said that they [9]........................... (hope) for a miracle to bring the money back.
Soon after the incident, the couple [10]........................... (cover) their windows with wire netting.

6 Read the story in Exercise 5 again. Find an example in 1–10 above of the following:

1 the simple past ....
2 the past continuous ....
3 the past perfect ....
4 an irregular past tense verb ....
5 a regular past tense verb ....

Skills

Reading

1 Read the interview with Dr. Andrew Wilson, an astronaut. Write the interviewer's questions (a–e, below) in the correct spaces.

1 ....
It was while I was watching the launch of a space shuttle in 1981 on TV. I was studying at college at that time and I thought to myself, "I would like to be on a space shuttle one day." So I decided to do some research. I sent a letter to NASA, and they replied and told me how to go about following my dreams!

2 ....
The first flight I made was to get used to space and the International Space Station. But what I really wanted to do was take a longer flight and stay on the station for a few months.

3 ....
They've always been very supportive, ever since I was a young boy. I used to read books from the library about being an astronaut when I was just a kid! So I don't think they were too surprised when I made the decision to become an astronaut.

4 ....
I've thought about this a lot. In my work I'm often away from my wife and children for long periods of time. But a mission to Mars would mean a very long separation, probably several years. I might consider it when my children have grown up and gone to college. But right now they are young, and I don't want to be away from them for so long.

5 ....
The main thing you'd need to do is study to become an engineer, scientist, or doctor. Then, after you've had some experience, you need to look for ways of doing space research. And then … it's over to you! Being an astronaut is the most amazing experience anyone can ever have.

a) What advice would you give to teenagers interested in being astronauts?
b) What was the first flight you ever took?
c) Have you ever considered going to Mars?
d) When did you decide that you wanted to be an astronaut?
e) What did your parents think about your career choice?

2 **Circle T (True) or F (False) for the sentences below.**

1 Andrew was in college in 1981. T / F
2 NASA gave him useful information about becoming an astronaut. T / F
3 His parents were shocked at his decision to become an astronaut. T / F
4 He hasn't decided yet whether or not he wants to go to Mars. T / F
5 You need to go to college before you can become an astronaut. T / F

Listening

10 **3** **Listen. What event is each speaker talking about?**

a) The *Challenger* space disaster in 1986

b) The first landing on the moon in 1969

11 **4** **Listen again and say what each speaker was doing when they heard about the event.**

	Event	**What was he/she doing?**
Speaker 1	....	....
	....	....
Speaker 2	....	....
	....	....

Writing for your Portfolio

5 **Think about an important event that you heard about. What were you doing at the time? Write a paragraph describing what you were doing and how you felt when you heard the news.**

UNIT 3 Shopping

12 **1 The underlined words are in the wrong place in the dialogue. Write them in the correct place. Then listen and check.**

Katie I love what you're wearing, Nicola! Have you been on a shopping <u>waste</u> [1]..? Everything's new!

Nicola Well, yes, everything's new to me, but none of these clothes are really new, if you know what I mean.

Katie Really? You mean they're <u>online</u> [2].. clothes? I'd never buy anything someone else has worn.

Nicola Well, you really <u>shouldn't</u> [3].. try it. Buying used things is a great way to recycle and save money. That's why I think online auction sites are such an amazing thing. I mean, it's such a <u>spree</u> [4].. buying new things all the time when you could easily reuse something else.

Katie I prefer paying for things in <u>debit card</u> [5].. , though. At least people can't get information about your bank account if you just hand over cash.

Nicola Oh, I think it's safe to tell your <u>cash</u> [6].. number to websites that have good security. But I agree, you <u>should</u> [7].. give that information to just anyone. Especially not <u>secondhand</u> [8].. . It can be very dangerous.

2 Write *Katie* or *Nicola*. Who ...

1 often buys recycled clothing? ....
2 doesn't trust debit cards? ....
3 buys things online? ....
4 prefers to pay in cash? ....

Saying what people ought to do

3 Match the sentences and the advice.

1 I never seem to have enough money.
2 My hair keeps falling into my eyes.
3 My computer keeps crashing.
4 I have a headache.
5 I think someone is using my bank account.

a) You should get someone to fix it.
b) You shouldn't read right now.
c) You should tell your bank immediately.
d) You should save more.
e) You should get it cut.

Language Focus

Vocabulary Money and shopping

1 Find words about shopping. Look up and down. Write the words next to their definitions.

1 bills or coins that you pay with

_ _ _ _

2 a special paper that you sign and pay with

_ _ _ _ _

3 shopping that you do on the Internet

_ _ _ _ _ _

4 things that aren't new are

_ _ _ _ _ _ hand

S C A S T R B E
A A S O S R E N
L S S P E D A S
C H E C K E N P
R O C C O B E R
E X O N L I N E
D E N O N T T E
I N D E B T E D
T I L L R I R

2 Match the pictures with the captions.

1 Can I pay by debit card? ....
2 It's very expensive. We can only afford to window shop here! ....
3 It's secondhand, but it looks brand new! ....
4 Sorry, we only take cash or cards, no checks. ....
5 Look at her! She's been on a shopping spree! ....

Talking about shopping

13 **3 Complete the dialogues with words and phrases from Exercises 1 and 2. Then listen and check.**

1 **Customer** These fit me really well. I'll take them. Can I pay by [1]........................?
Salesclerk Sorry, it's [2]........................ only. No checks or cards.

2 **Will** What an amazing jacket!
Amy I know. It's a genuine 1950s one. I found it in a [3]........................ store.

3 **Caitlin** I hope you're not taking me on a [4]........................ . I don't have any money.
Carrie Neither do I, but we can always [5]........................ .

Grammar

Should(n't) / ought

1 Match the problems and the advice.

1 I keep losing my keys!
2 I can't see the board in class.
3 I get an earache after listening to my MP3 player.
4 I feel bad about being so rude to Mandy.

a) You should apologize.
b) You should keep them in a safe place.
c) You shouldn't play it so loud.
d) You ought to have your eyes tested.

2 Complete the sentences with *should, shouldn't*, or *ought*.

1 **A** I have a toothache.
B You .... eat so much candy.
2 **A** I bought these pants a week ago and the zipper is already broken!
B You .... to take them back to the store.
3 **A** I'd really like to see *The Golden Compass*.
B I think you .... read the book first.
4 **A** My parents don't want me to go to the concert.
B I really don't think you .... to go.
5 **A** I have a temperature and a bad cough.
B Maybe you .... go to school today.

3 Rewrite the second sentence so that it has the same meaning as the first. Use the words in parentheses.

1 It's a good idea to get to the show early. (should)
We .... early.
2 It isn't a good idea to eat candy. (shouldn't)
You .... candy.
3 Watching movies in English can help you improve. (ought to)
You .... movies in English to improve.
4 It's rude to interrupt people when they're talking. (shouldn't)
You .... people when they're talking.
5 The best thing to do is ask the teacher to help you. (should)
You .... the teacher to help you.
6 A doctor is the person to see when you are sick. (ought to)
You .... when you are sick.

Gerunds

4 **Complete the description using the words below.**

being cleaning coming performing playing teaching

Cleaner becomes professional guitarist

[1]............................ a song on a classical guitar one day has led to an Hispanic cleaner's new career as a guitar teacher.
A webcam filmed the man, who had a job [2]............................ offices and floors at a state university.
The president of the university then invited him to play at events around the campus.

Since then, his achievements have included [3]............................ on stage and [4]............................ classical guitar to students.
The man said that he became a cleaner after [5]............................ to the U.S., although [6]............................ a classical guitarist was always his lifelong dream.

5 **Complete the sentences with the gerund form of the verbs in parentheses.**

1 I have to clean the house on the weekends. .... the garbage out is the worst job! (take)
2 Michael loves .... He wants to go to drama school one day. (act)
3 .... for clothes is Jessie's favorite activity. (shop)
4 I don't think .... money on expensive designer clothes is worth it. (spend)
5 I hate .... My cakes are always a disaster! (bake)
6 It can be hard to get used to .... in a city. (drive)

6 **Read Holly's answers. Then complete the sentences.**

Do you .... ?	
play a musical instrument	*Yes, I play piano. I practice every day.*
listen to music	*Yes, all the time. I love it.*
jog in the park	*No, I hate it.*
clean the house	*Yes, I clean my room every day.*
shop for clothes	*Yes, I love it!*

Holly's regular activities include [1]................................ the piano, [2]................................ to music, [3]................................ her room, and [4]................................ for clothes. She doesn't like [5]................................ in the park.

Skills

Listening

14 **1** **Complete the dialogue using the words below. Then listen and check.**

debit card   window-shopping   cash   check   online

Sarah What are you looking for on the Internet?

Connor I'm looking for a copy of an old book I used to have as a child. But it looks like it's out of print now. None of the bookstores have it.

Sarah You should try an online auction site. I bet you'll find several copies of it there.

Connor I've never bought anything [1]............................... before.

Sarah You should try it! You can find some amazing things!

Connor How do you pay for things? You can't pay in [2]..............................., can you?

Sarah Well, you usually have to give your [3]............................... number to make an online payment. But some sellers don't mind if you write them a [4]............................. . And, if you find someone who lives near you, you could even go and pick up the item and buy it with cash.

Connor Don't you have to be over 18 to register, though?

Sarah Yes. If you're younger than that, you should ask your parents to shop with you. Anyone can browse though! Come on, let's do some [5]............................... online in the meantime!

Reading

2 **Read the article and then match the sentence halves.**

A Life for Sale

John Freyer, a student at the University of Iowa, decided to sell everything he owned on the Internet. He and his friends tagged all his possessions and put them up for sale on an auction website to be sold to the highest bidder. "I invited about 50 people to my house for an 'inventory party,'" said Freyer. The items included an unopened box of taco shells, half a bottle of mouthwash, his clothes, and even unopened presents for his family.

Before long, Freyer's possessions found new homes all over the world. A chair ended up in the Museum of Modern Art. A bag of pork skins went to Japan. Then Freyer had another idea. He decided to track down and then visit his old possessions in their new homes.

After that, he wrote a book about his project. It is called *All My Life for Sale*. It tells the story of Freyer's life, his travels, and his thoughts about the objects in our lives.

He still keeps track of his old things and where they have ended up. On the website allmylifeforsale.com you can see where many of Freyer's belongings ended up. But of course, he doesn't own that website. It was his last possession to be sold.

1 John Freyer
2 He sold
3 His clothes, everyday objects, and presents
4 After he sold his things, he
5 The last thing he sold
6 He is keeping track

a) went to visit them.
b) of what happened to his belongings after he sold them.
c) was his website.
d) everything he had online.
e) decided to sell everything he owned.
f) were included in the sale.

3 Find words in the article that mean ...

1 belongings ....
2 a sale to someone who pays the highest price ....
3 put price tags on ....
4 a list of property ....
5 someone who takes part in a sale where something is sold for the highest price ....
6 discover ....

Writing for your Portfolio

4 Imagine you are selling all your belongings online. Write a web page describing your life.

Paragraph 1: Give some background information about yourself.
Paragraph 2: Briefly describe your home, your town, and your free-time activities under three separate headings.
Paragraph 3: Say why you think your life would be a good thing for someone to buy!

UNIT 4 A working life

15 **1 Complete the dialogue using the words below. Then listen and check.**

before	creative	going	hardworking	honest
college	soon as	taking	when	working with

Jon What are you going to do [1]........................ we graduate?
Beth Well, as [2]........................ we finish, I'm [3]........................ a vacation.
Jon Where are you going?
Beth I'm [4]........................ to Chile. I think it's important to see another country [5]........................ I go to college.
Jon Where will you go to [6]........................ ?
Beth I'm going to our state college to study to be a vet!
Jon You'd make a good vet. You are kind and patient. I think that's important when you're [7]........................ people or animals. I couldn't do a job like that. I wonder what my ideal job would be.
Beth You should think about working in advertising or something, since you're so [8]........................ .
Jon But I'm not sure I'm [9]........................ enough. I'm pretty lazy.
Beth Well, at least you're [10]........................ !

2 Match these people and their ideal jobs.

1 Nikita would be a good nurse
2 Paul should be a writer
3 Marek would be good at sales
4 Jessica should go into business
5 I think Isabel could easily work on her own
6 Ben could be a company president in a few years

a) because she's responsible and efficient.
b) because she likes helping people.
c) because she's very independent.
d) because he's hardworking and very ambitious.
e) because he's good at persuading people.
f) because he's imaginative and creative.

Saying what you want to do

16 **3 Number the lines in the correct order. Then listen and check.**

Rosie .... I could never be a doctor.
Rosie .... I hate blood! Don't you?
Rosie .... I'm not sure yet, but I'm thinking of becoming an architect.
Rosie .... Well, I like design, and I'm good at math, too.
Sean .... Is there any job you'd never want to do?
Sean .... No, I don't mind it. I could be a doctor, I guess …
Sean .... What do you think you'd like about that?
Sean .....1..... What job do you want to do one day?
Sean .... Why not?

Language Focus

Vocabulary Personality adjectives

1 Read the notes interviewers have made about a group of college applicants. Answer the questions.

Student
A – calm, never in a rush
B – determined to get to the top quickly
C – wants to help whenever possible
D – very direct, doesn't say things that aren't true
E – will work very hard
F – relaxed, casual, not bossy

Which student is ... ?

1 easygoing ....
2 helpful ....
3 patient ....
4 hardworking ....
5 ambitious ....
6 honest ....

2 Write the opposites of these adjectives in the correct column.

ambitious creative efficient friendly helpful
honest imaginative kind patient polite

un	*im*	*dis*	*in*

Talking about personalities and jobs

3 Complete the sentences with the opposites of the underlined adjectives.

1 I could never be a waiter. I'm too <u>rude</u> and <u>unfriendly</u>!
To be a waiter, you have to be .... and ....
2 I could never be a farmer and get up early for work. I'm too <u>lazy</u>.
You have to be .... to be a farmer.
3 It's hard to imagine Ellen being a coach. She's so <u>impatient</u>.
You have to be .... to be a good coach.
4 I can't believe Annie's going to be a teacher. She's so <u>unkind</u> to children!
Teachers should be .... to children.
5 He shouldn't be a police officer. He's <u>not truthful</u> all the time.
Police officers need to be .... people.

Grammar

Talking about the future
be going to present continuous (review)

1 Complete the sentences. Use *be going to* or the present continuous.

1 I hate my hair. I .... it cut. (get)

2 I've just called the salon. Wish me luck! I .... it cut tomorrow afternoon. (have)

3 John's .... a speech at his sister's wedding next month. (give)

4 He .... an expensive suit. (rent)

5 I .... to New York tomorrow. (fly) It's .... 12 hours! (take)

6 I .... an exam this afternoon. (take) I know I .... well. (do)

2 Which sentences ...

1 ... are about someone's intentions? ....

2 ... are about fixed arrangements in the future? ....

3 Complete the dialogue with *be going to* or the present continuous of the verbs in parentheses.

Sarah I really like Mark. I want to get to know him better.

Jade So what are you going to do?

Sarah Well, I have an idea. I [1]................................ (invite) him to the concert.

Jade What concert?

Sarah Don't you know? I sing in a band, and we [2]................................ (play) at the dance tomorrow night. Why don't you come too?

Jade I can't. Tomorrow we [3]................................ (rehearse) for the school play.

Sarah What time does it finish? You could join us later. We [4]................................ (go) to a restaurant after the concert. It's [5]................................ (be) a lot of fun!

Jade Who [6]................................ (go)?

Sarah Just the band—and Mark—I hope!

Future time clauses

4 **Circle the correct option.**

1 *As soon as/Before you* travel to the U.S., you need to get a passport.
2 I always have a snack *after/before* getting home from school.
3 What are you doing *before/when* school finishes today?
4 *As soon as/ When* it rains, we have P.E. inside.
5 I'm going to get my driver's license *as soon as/after* I can.

5 **Complete the second sentence so that it has a similar meaning to the first sentence. Use one of the words or phrases in the box below.**

after   as soon as   before   when

1 *The exact moment* I get home, I'll call you.
I'll call you .... I get home.
2 I'll definitely visit the Taj Mahal *at the time* I go to India.
.... I go to India, I'll definitely visit the Taj Mahal.
3 Are you going to study again *at an earlier time than* your final exams?
Are you going to study again .... your final exams?
4 What are we going to do *when* the finals *are finished*?
What are we going to do .... finals?

6 **Complete the sentences with the correct form of the verbs in parentheses.**

1 I .... you a postcard when I .... to Florida. (send, get)
2 Promise me you .... me as soon as you .... the news. (call, hear)
3 What .... after you .... school? (you do, finish)
4 .... your dinner before you .... out, please. (finish, go)
5 If you .... your tickets online, it .... as expensive. (book, not be)
6 When you .... Carl again, ... him I said "hello". (see, tell)

7 **Write five sentences using the future time clauses from Exercise 4.**

1 ....
2 ....
3 ....
4 ....
5 ....

Skills

Listening

17 **1** **Listen to the radio show about people's summer jobs. Write the number of the speaker next to the correct photo.**

A

a) testing movie DVDs

B

b) testing computer games

C

c) testing recipes

D

d) playing historical characters

E

e) making cotton candy at a zoo

Reading

2 **Read the article and answer the questions.**

You need to have a head for heights

Being fired doesn't bother Áron Molnar. In fact, it's part of his daily job.
That's because Áron is a human cannonball. Twice a day in the busy season, he flies out of a mouth of a cannon and through the air into a safety net at the other side of the circus ring.
Áron has always been close to the circus. His Hungarian parents met while they were both part of a circus, so becoming a circus performer was a natural choice of career for Áron. He started as an acrobat and trapeze artist, but he always wanted to be the human cannonball. As soon as there was a vacancy, he applied for the job.
It isn't an easy job, though. "There's more to my job than just climbing into the cannon and waiting for the burst of air that will send me flying," he says. "I have to fly straight, keep my body completely still, and then do a somersault in midair, so that I can land on my back in the net. All this has to be done in just two seconds!"

This is not a job for people who want to earn a lot of money. Yes, the actual working hours are much shorter than a normal nine-to-five job, but you have to live and move around with the circus, and although your act may last for only a few minutes, you have to be involved in the whole show, at every performance. You have to be physically strong, too. Áron spends several hours every day working on exercises to strengthen his knees and back. Every flight is a risk. One wrong move and there could be a very serious accident.
Is it worth the risk? Áron says, "Every time I work, I feel free, it's as if I'm flying. How many people can say that about their job?"

1 Why was Áron's career choice not unexpected? ....
2 Why would gymnastics training be useful in this job? ....
3 Why does he have to be strong? ....
4 Why is Áron's job risky? ....
5 What does Áron say he feels every time he works? ....

Writing for your Portfolio

3 **Read the advertisement. Write a letter saying why you want this job and what qualities and experience you have that make you suitable.**

Students! Are you looking for summer work?

Are you:

helpful, patient, kind, and friendly?
efficient and responsible?
hardworking?
creative and imaginative?

Club U.S. is looking for students aged 16-18 to work in a number of areas such as catering, working with pets and children, and working in arts at its international summer camps for children from the ages of 5 to 10.

UNIT 5 Bookworms

18 **1 Complete the dialogue using the words below. Then listen and check.**

boring	find out	get into	great	hang out
no way	put it down	so	such	turn into

Joe You want to do something tonight? We could play tennis or just [1]......................... at the gym.

Lucy Sorry, I'd rather stay in and read my book.

Joe That sounds so [2] .... ! You're always reading these days. You're going to [3] .... a real bookworm!

Lucy But it's such a [4] .... book. It's *Point Blanc*, the second Alex Rider book. Really, it's [5]......................... exciting, I just can't [6]......................... !

Joe What's it about?

Lucy Alex Rider has to pretend he's someone else, a boy named Alex Friend. His mission is to go to Point Blanc, a school for spoiled rich kids, in order to [7]......................... what's really going on there. He learns that it's a very strange place, with a lot of strange things happening … It's just [8]......................... a good book that I just don't want it to end.

Joe I enjoyed the first Alex Rider book. Even though it took me a while to [9]......................... , it was really good. This one sounds even better. Can I take a look at it?

Lucy [10]......................... , I'm still reading it!

2 Answer the questions.

1 What does Joe want to do?

....

2 Why doesn't Lucy want to stop reading?

....

3 What does Joe think of her plans to read instead of going to the gym?

....

4 What does Alex Rider discover at Point Blanc?

....

5 What did Joe think of the first Alex Rider book?

....

6 Why doesn't Lucy hand over the book to Joe?

....

Language Focus

Vocabulary Kinds of books

1 **Match the book reviews 1–6 with the kinds of books a–f.**

1 As usual, the sharp-eyed Private Investigator finds out that everyone has a motive for the murder. She uncovers all sorts of secrets in everyone's lives ....

2 This informative book tells us all about the life of Martin Luther King, Jr., from his birth in January 1929 in Atlanta, Georgia, in the South of the U.S. ....

3
O mother, mother, make my bed,
O make it soft and narrow:
My love has died for me today,
I'll die for him tomorrow.

4 The first few explore the themes of childhood and growing up seen through the eyes of a child. Finally, in the last one, "Behind the Bike Racks," the narrator is a teenager in high school.

5 Chapter 11: *Trouble shooting*
Make sure your digital camera is connected to the computer via the special USB provided. If this is not done, you will not be able to see the icon on the screen ....

6 Sadly, Lucinda stood on the bridge, looking down at the water as it flowed past her. And suddenly, he was there. Their eyes met across the reflections in the river. Lucinda knew he was the one she would marry.

a) biography ....
b) detective novel ....
c) nonfiction ....
d) poetry ....
e) romance ....
f) short story collection ....

Talking about books

19 **2** **Complete the dialogue using the words below. Then listen and check.**

alright	detective	do you like	exciting
favorite	find out	like	love

Cameron [1].. comic books?
Evie Do you mean *Batman*, or something like that?
Cameron Yes. It's my [2].. kind of book.
Evie Hmm, they're [3].. , but I'm not crazy about them.
Cameron So what do you [4].. ?
Evie I like books that are [5].. , where you just can't wait to [6].. what happens in the end.
Cameron Do you like [7].. novels and crime stories?
Evie Yes, I [8].. that kind of book.

Grammar

So / such

1 Match the sentence halves.

1 Mrs. Green was so angry about the test scores
2 She drove so fast
3 The test was so difficult
4 She was so hungry
5 It was such an emotional play
6 She was such a good author

a) that she skidded and crashed.
b) that I couldn't answer any questions.
c) that she ate all her food in about two minutes.
d) that she gave us all extra homework.
e) that everyone wanted to read her books.
f) that everyone felt exhausted by the time it was over.

2 Circle the correct word.

1 It was *so/such* cold weather that they decided to close the school for the day.
2 The trip was *so/such* long that I wanted to sleep most of the way.
3 They gave me *so/such* a bad haircut that I won't ever go back there again.
4 I have *so/such* a lot of homework that I won't be able to go to bed before midnight.
5 The book was *so/such* boring that I didn't even finish it.
6 The movie was *so/such* sad that I spent most of the time in tears.

3 Add *so...that* or *such...that* and write sentences about the pictures.

1 He is / in love / he / walk / into a streetlight.

....

....

2 She / ate / fast / she / has / a stomachache.

....

....

3 It is / a big package / it / not fit / in the mailbox.

....

....

Phrasal verbs

4 **Write the correct meaning of the verb + preposition at the end of each sentence.**

1 Can you turn up the volume please? I can't hear it. ....
2 I wonder how many people will turn up at the event? ....
3 I wasn't looking and I ran into a tree!. ....
4 I ran into an old friend yesterday. ....
5 As soon as you get into the taxi, tell the driver where you want to go. ....
6 It's difficult to start a new book, but you'll soon get into it. ....

enter
attend
become used to
met by accident
increase
hit

5 **Complete the sentences with the correct form of the phrasal verbs below.**

take care of | look into | play around | run after

1 The police .... the robber, but they couldn't catch him.
2 "Stop .... , class, and finish your work!" said the teacher.
3 I'm not sure whether it will be possible to get tickets, but I'll .... it this afternoon.
4 You can borrow my MP3 player, but please .... it.

6 **Circle the correct word.**

1 It's a good idea to check *over/around* your work again before you turn it in.
2 I have to have a tooth taken *off/out*.
3 She's finding it hard to get *up/over* her grandmother's death.
4 There's so much to learn, I'm not sure I can take it all *up/in*.
5 What's the best way to put *away/out* a fire?
6 The surgeon is carrying *on/out* an operation this afternoon.

7 **Replace the underlined expressions with the phrasal verbs below.**

break up | find out | get over | put up | take after

1 Who do you resemble most in your family? ....
2 I'm trying to get information about tickets for the next game. ....
3 I'm sorry to hear you have a cold. I hope you recover from it soon. ....
4 To get more publicity for our show, we should display posters around the school. ....
5 I don't want to end our relationship because of what happened. ....

Skills

Reading

1 Read these book reviews on a website. How many people didn't like the book?

The End is the 13th and last book in *A Series of Unfortunate Events*, a set of books written by Lemony Snicket. It tells the story of the Baudelaire orphans. This is a great book. It's probably my favorite book ever. My only complaint is that this is the last one!
Gina

I thought the book was written in a rushed sort of way. It jumped around so much that it was sometimes difficult to know what exactly was going on. The details weren't all that good, but I still enjoyed it, although it's not the superstar book that everyone said it was. This book talks about other books in the series too much. And the story was very odd. I found it impossible to read!
Ronin

I took this book out from the library, thinking from the plot and the title that it would be good. But the story is very jerky, it skips around a lot, and at the end of the book, I wasn't sure what it was all about. A lot of the things the orphans did were far from believable. This book is OK, but not the greatest book I've ever read.
Tyler

This book is my favorite book. I couldn't stop reading it. The ending was moving. The book answered a lot of questions for me, but also left some questions unanswered. It was AMAZING!
Sophie

This book looked like it would be exciting, but it wasn't. I was very disappointed, because after only four chapters, I was already so bored with it that I didn't care what happened to any of the characters. I kept thinking it would get better, but I was wrong.
Abbie

At first it didn't really interest me. Then I started getting into it more. And I couldn't stop! I read it in around two days: now I wish I had taken more time to read it because I just didn't want it to end. It's the best book I've ever read. It was heartbreaking to finish it. I wish there was a sequel to this book.
Amina

2 **Read the reviews again and write the name of ...**

1 two readers who complain there isn't a sequel. ....
2 two readers who found the book confusing to follow. ....
3 two readers who rate the book as the best they've ever read. ....
4 one reader who thought the story wasn't very unusual. ....
5 two readers who thought the story was unusual. ....
6 two readers who couldn't put the book down. ....

3 **Write the underlined words from the reviews next to the correct meaning:**

1 a book that continues the story of an earlier book ....
2 emotional, leading to intense feelings ....
3 strange, not ordinary ....
4 unconnected ....
5 very sad ....

Listening

20 **4** **Listen to the conversation and check (✓) the answers for Luke and Ashley.**

What do you think about reading? (Check one box for each statement.)

	Strongly agree	Agree	Disagree	Strongly disagree
1 Reading is more for girls than boys.	Luke ☐ Ashley ☐	Luke ☐ Ashley ☐	Luke ☐ Ashley ☐	Luke ☐ Ashley ☐
2 Reading is boring.	Luke ☐ Ashley ☐	Luke ☐ Ashley ☐	Luke ☐ Ashley ☐	Luke ☐ Ashley ☐
3 Reading is important.	Luke ☐ Ashley ☐	Luke ☐ Ashley ☐	Luke ☐ Ashley ☐	Luke ☐ Ashley ☐
4 I can't find books that interest me.	Luke ☐ Ashley ☐	Luke ☐ Ashley ☐	Luke ☐ Ashley ☐	Luke ☐ Ashley ☐
5 I would be happy if someone gave me a book as a present.	Luke ☐ Ashley ☐	Luke ☐ Ashley ☐	Luke ☐ Ashley ☐	Luke ☐ Ashley ☐

Writing for your Portfolio

5 **Complete the questionnaire yourself. Then use it to write a paragraph about your reading habits. Explain why you agree or disagree with each statement.**

UNIT 6 The main event

21 **1 Complete the dialogue using the words and phrases below. Then listen and check.**

move	are you allowed	aren't allowed to	forbidden
let	goes off	shouldn't	return

Kiah Martin tells me you're going to a 3D show at the iMax theater next week. It's really cool! You'll love it. I went last month.

Oscar Oh, good, then I can ask you about it. [1]........................ to take pictures during the show?

Kiah No, they don't [2]........................ you use any cameras at all. Cameras are [4]........................ in the auditorium by law.

Oscar What about food? Are there any rules about that?

Kiah Well, you [4]........................ eat in the auditorium. But you can buy refreshments just outside, once the show is over. The other thing to remember is that you have to [5]........................ your glasses. If you don't return them, an alarm [6]........................! You also [7]........................ talk too loud. Oh, and some people think the seats [8]........................ during a show, but they don't.

Oscar Right! I'll remember all that.

22 **2 Listen again. Which of the following are allowed? Write A (allowed) or NA (not allowed).**

1 using a video camera ....
2 taking pictures ....
3 eating candy in the auditorium ....
4 wearing 3D glasses ....
6 talk softly ....
7 drinking soda while you watch the movie ....
8 eating popcorn afterward ....

Talking about permission

3 Look at the rules. Then complete the answers to the questions. Use *allowed to*.

1 Why don't you take your cell phone?
We .... cell phones.
2 Why don't you wear earrings to school?
We .... to school.
3 Why don't you take your dog to school?
Dogs .... at school.
4 Why can't you take this book out of the library?
You .... home.
5 Why don't you ever wear your baseball cap to school?
We .... hats in school.

No hats allowed in school.

No jewelry in school.

No cell phones.

No pets.

These books can only be used in the library.

Language Focus

Vocabulary Special events

1 Circle the correct word to make phrases which describe special events.

1 a book *fair/tournament*
2 a car *show/museum*
3 a bike *fair/race*
4 a fashion *race/show*
5 a movie *exhibition/premiere*
6 a music *festival/night*
7 a school *fair/night*
8 a tennis *tournament/festival*

2 Write the number of the correct event from Exercise 1 in each photo.

a

b

c

d

e

f

g

h

Talking about events

23 **3 Number the lines in the correct order. Then listen and check.**

A .... Yeah, I love them, too. What about a fashion show? Have you ever been to one?
A .....*1*..... Have you ever been to a music festival?
A .... What were they like?
A .... What was it like?
B .... Really interesting. I think modeling must be hard work though.
B .... Yes, I went to Bonnaroo last year. I saw the Raconteurs play.
B .... Amazing. They're my favorite band.
B .... Yeah, my cousin's a model, so she got me a ticket once.

Grammar

The passive

1 Complete the sentences using the words below.

(not) allow attend hold play spend wear

1 Every year, a lot of money .... on music festivals around the world.
2 In a tennis tournament, a game of doubles .... by four players.
3 The latest fashions .... by models at a fashion show.
4 The World Series .... every year in North America.
5 The premiere of the movie .... by movie stars and celebrities.
6 Children .... in the pool without an adult.

2 Complete the opening lines of these newspaper articles with the past passive.

1 **Police arrest robber**

A robber .... by police last night...

2 **Air ambulance flies pop star to hospital**

A pop star .... to the hospital yesterday...

3 **Retired man wins race**

Yesterday, the annual 20km fun run ....by a man aged 72.

4 **Oscar Award for Hilary Swank**

Hilary Swank .... the Oscar for Best Actress at last night's LA ceremony.

5 **City elects new mayor**

The new mayor for the city .... last night...

6 **Millions watch the Super Bowl**

The Super Bowl .... by millions of people around the world on Saturday.

3 Complete the description with the present passive or past passive form of the verbs in parentheses.

Early tennis balls [1].......................... (make) in Scotland from sheep stomachs. These tennis balls [2].......................... usually [3].......................... (stuff) with wool from the animal. In the 18th century, strips of wool [4].......................... (wrap) tightly around into a little ball. Then string [5].......................... (tie) around the ball and the whole ball [6].......................... (cover) with a white cloth. Modern tennis balls [7].......................... (make) from rubber. They [8].......................... then [9].......................... (cover) with a soft material called felt.

Make / let / be allowed to

4 **Complete the sentences with the correct form of *make, let,* or *allow*.**

1 Are you .... to go out late at night?
2 What time do your parents .... you come home?
3 Do your parents .... you to play computer games in your bedroom?
4 Will you .... me borrow your laptop this weekend?
5 We aren't .... to wear jewelry to school.
6 I'm so tired. Our P.E. teacher .... us run for an hour!
7 My parents won't .... me to miss any school unless I'm sick.
8 I can't drink coffee. It .... me stay up all night.

5 **Read the rules and complete the speech bubbles with the correct form of *make, let, allow,* or *not allow*.**

Welcome to the **Life in the Middle Ages** weekend! To discover how people lived long ago, there are certain rules we have to follow:

1 No electronic games, since they weren't even invented then!
2 No makeup.
3 No cell phones, but you can use the pay phone in the reception area.
4 No radios. Entertainment in the Middle Ages included acting and singing and dancing. So get ready to entertain us!
5 No showers, although you may take a bath.
6 No single rooms. We have to share, four to a tent.

1 They didn't .... me play my computer game!
2 We weren't .... to wear makeup.
3 They didn't .... us to use cell phones. But they .... us use the pay phone.
4 They didn't .... us listen to radios. They .... us sing, act, and dance!
5 We weren't .... to use the shower, but we were .... to take a bath.
6 They .... us share tents.

6 **Write sentences about these signs. Use *(not) allow* and the verbs below.**

dive | eat and drink | park | ride your bike

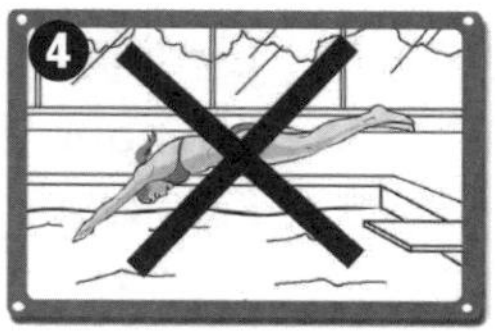

1 You .... in the auditorium.
2 You .... here.
3 You .... for one hour.
4 You .... here.

Skills

Reading

1 **Read the description below quickly. What kind of text is it?**

a) an email b) a blog c) a magazine article

Tom Wilkinson

MONDAY, July 6

As most of you know, I don't like running. I never go jogging, and I wouldn't run a marathon even if I was paid for it. But one thing that would make me run for my life, literally, would be if there were several hundred bulls chasing me.

Tomorrow, that's exactly what people are coming here to do. I'm at the annual San Fermin Fiesta in Pamplona, Spain. This festival began in the Middle Ages, and has grown in popularity ever since. It lasts for a week in July, when the city is transformed into an ocean of red and white, the official colors of the festival.

Before the bullring was built, bull fights were held in a large square in the city. The custom of running ahead of the bulls started when the bulls had to be moved from the outskirts of the city to the bullring. Some of the customs have changed over the years, but certain things are still the same.

Anyone who wants to participate in the run has to enter the special area by 7:30 a.m. The gates are then closed, and they won't be opened to let you leave after that. At just before 8:00 a.m. the runners ask the statue of San Fermin to protect them. At eight o'clock, two rockets are fired. With the first rocket, the gates of the bull enclosure are opened, and with the second, the bulls are set free to run. They chase after the runners down the length of the bull run, which is about 800 meters. The whole thing lasts about two minutes.

It sounds easier than it is. You can't just run straight ahead. The route goes up and down narrow streets, with few places for runners to hide except doorways of buildings. The end of the run, just before the bulls enter the ring, is one of the most dangerous spots. People running with the bulls have fallen here, and have been injured (sometimes fatally).

Don't worry if you're reading this, Mom. No one under the age of 18 is allowed to participate. I'll be watching from the safety of the balcony!

2 **Circle T (True) or F (False) for the sentences below. Correct the false sentences.**

1 Tom has gone to Pamplona to run in the fiesta. T / F

....

2 The fiesta is a lot more than 100 years old. T / F ....

3 The fiesta starts on July 7. T / F ....

4 Once you have decided to run in the fiesta, you aren't allowed to change your mind. T / F

....

5 There are many places to hide from the bulls in the narrow streets. T / F

....

6 The race gets easier toward the end. T / F ....

7 Anyone can take part. T / F ....

8 Tom knows his mother might be reading this blog. T / F ....

3 **Find words in the blog that mean:**

1 a race of about 42 km ....

2 changed ....

3 legally recognized and allowed ....

4 edges ....

5 traditions ....

6 fenced area ....

7 in a deadly way ....

8 take part ....

Listening

24 **4** **Listen to Part 1. Where is the speaker?**

a) a music festival b) a fashion show c) a school fair d) a sports event

25 **5** **Listen to Part 2 and answer the questions.**

1 Where is the event held? ....

2 Where is the speaker staying? ....

3 How did he get a ticket? ....

4 What did his parents want him to do instead? ....

5 Why did they let him go eventually? ....

Writing for your Portfolio

6 **Write a short description of an event you have been to.**

- What kind of event was it?
- When and where was it held?
- What did you do there?
- What was it like?

Wordlist

Unit 1

beliefs /bə'lifs/
boxes /'baksɪz/
colony /'kaləni/
corn /kɔrn/
fight /faɪt/
gloves /glʌvz/
goggles /'gagəlz/
harbor /'harbər/
harvest /'harvəst/
helmet /'hɛlmət/
incredible /ɪn'krɛdəbəl/
merchants /'mɛrchənts/
native /'neɪtɪv/
pads /pædz/
port /pɔrt/
shorts /ʃɔrts/
sneakers /'snikərz
socks /saks/
steep hill /ˌstip 'hɪl/
successful /sək'sɛsfəl/
to be lucky /ˌbi 'lʌki/
to belong /bɪ'laŋ/
to chase /'ʧeɪs/
to end up /ˌɛnd 'ʌp/
to grow corn /ˌgroʊ 'kɔrn/
to pay taxes /ˌpeɪ 'tæksəz/
to roll /'roʊl/
to take part /ˌteɪk 'part/
turkey /'tərki/
vest /vɛst/

Unit 2

bottom /'batəm/
deepest /'dipɪst/
disgusting /dɪs'gʌstɪŋ/
flight /flaɪt/
grade /greɪd/
height /haɪt/
millions /'mɪ(l)yənz/
plaque /plæk/
quiet /'kwaɪət/
rocket /'rakət/
seat /sit/
space shuttle /'speɪs ˌʃʌtəl/
sunrise /'sʌnraɪz/
sunset /'sʌnset/
to break up /ˌbreɪk 'ʌp/
to carry /'kæri/
to get into /ˌgɛt 'ɪntu/
to land /'lænd/
to race /'reɪs/
to reenter /ri'ɛntər/
to risk /'rɪsk/
to run out of something /ˌrʌn 'aʊt əv ˌ.../
to set out /ˌsɛt 'aʊt/
to soak /'soʊk/
to step /'stɛp/
to strike /'straɪk/
top /tap/
vehicles /'viəkləz/
weird /wɪrd/

Unit 3

asteroid /'æstəˌrɔɪd/
brand new /ˌbrænd 'nu/
burning process /'bərnɪŋ ˌprasəs/
challenge /'ʧæləndʒ/
change /ʧeɪndʒ/
credit card /'krɛdɪt ˌkard/
debit card /'dɛbɪt ˌkard/
engine /'ɛndʒən/
exhausted /ɪg'zɔstəd/
fear /fɪr/
fuel /'fyu(ə)l/
high-pressure gas /ˌhaɪ ˌprɛʃər 'gæs/
hose /hoʊz/
launch /lɔnʧ/
leather /'leðər/
lifestyle /'laɪfstaɪl/
mass /mæs/
secondhand section /ˌsɛkənd'hænd ˌsekʃən/
temperature /'tɛmp(ə)rəʧur/
tiring /'taɪrɪŋ/
to cut up /ˌkʌt 'ʌp/
to exchange /ɪks'ʧeɪndʒ/
to load /'loʊd/
to solve a problem /ˌsalv ə 'prabləm/
to suppose /sə'poʊz/
to waste /weɪst/
to weigh /'weɪ/
wages /'weɪdʒəz/

Unit 4

ambitious /æm'bɪʃəs/
arrogant /'ærəgənt/
creative /kri'eɪtɪv/
customers /'kʌstəmərz/
dishwasher /'dɪʃwaʃər/
easygoing /ˌizi 'goʊɪŋ/
efficient /ɪ'fɪʃənt/
friendly /'frɛndli/
hardworking /ˌhard'wərkɪŋ/
helpful /'hɛlpfəl/
honest /'anəst/
imaginative /ɪ'mædʒnətɪv/
independent /ˌɪndə'pɛndə nt/
kind /kaɪnd/
ladder /'lædər/
morning /'mɔrnɪŋ/
patient /'peɪʃənt/
peacekeeping force / 'piskipɪŋ ˌfɔrs/
polite /pə'laɪt/
responsible /rɪ'span(t)səbəl/
soldier /'soʊldʒər/
the sight of /ðə 'saɪt əv/
to get ready /ˌget 'rɛdi/
to involve /ɪn'valv/
to lose /luz/
to make jokes /ˌmeɪk 'dʒoʊks/
window washer /'wɪndoʊ ˌwaʃər/

Unit 5

breeding grounds /'bridɪŋ ˌgraʊndz/
bright /braɪt/
confusing /kən'fyuzɪŋ/
creatures /'kriʧərz/
currents /'kʌrənts/
daylight /'deɪlaɪt/
disappointed / dɪsə'pɔɪntəd/
dream /drim/
ending /'ɛndɪŋ/
eyesight /'aɪsaɪt/
parachute /'pærəʃut/
plankton /'plæŋktən/
predators /'prɛdətərz/
series /'sɪriz/
steam /stim/
thrilling /'θrɪlɪŋ/
to burn /bərn/
to care about something /'ker əbaʊt .../
to cram into something /'kræm ˌɪntə .../
to fall asleep /fɔl ə'slip/
to feed /fid/
to give birth /ˌgɪv 'bərθ/
to hang out /ˌhæŋ 'aʊt/
to hurtle /'hərtəl/
to insist /ɪn'sɪst/
to jolt /'dʒoʊlt/
to knock over something /'nak ˌoʊvər .../
to lay eggs /ˌleɪ 'ɛgz/
to migrate /'maɪgreɪt/
to pick /pɪk/
to put something down /ˌpʊt ˌ... 'daʊn/
to recommend /ˌrɛkə'mɛnd/
to run into someone /'rʌn ˌɪntə .../
to stand up /ˌstænd 'ʌp/
to take after someone /'teɪk ˌæftər .../
to take up something /'teɪk ˌʌp .../
to turn up the volume /tərn ˌʌp ðə 'valyəm/
view /vyu/
walk out /ˌwɔk 'aʊt/
waterfalls /'wɔtərfɔlz/

Unit 6

bike race /'baɪk ˌreɪs/
book fair /'bʊk ˌfɛr)/
car show /'kar ˌʃoʊ/
fashion show /'fæʃən ˌʃoʊ/
fireworks /'faɪ(ə)rwərks/

front page /ˌfrʌnt ˈpeɪʤ/

movie premiere /ˈmuvi prɪmɪr/

put up the tent /pʊt ˌʌp ðə ˈtɛnt/

rock festival /ˈrɑk ˌfɛstɪvəl/

school fair /ˌskul ˈfɛr/

strawberries /ˈstrɔˌbɛriz/

tennis tournament /ˈtɛnɪs ˌtʊrnəmənt/

to camp /kæmp/

to pick up /ˌpɪk ˈʌp/

to stay overnight /ˌsteɪ oʊvərˈnaɪt/

Pronunciation guide

Vowels

/i/	real, screen
/ɪ/	dish, sit
/ɛ/	chess, bed
/æ/	bad, taxi
/ʌ/	must, done
/ʊ/	good, full
/u/	choose, view
/ə/	dramatic, the
/ɑ/	stop, opera
/ɔ/	saw, daughter

Vowels + /r/

/ər/	first, shirt
/ɑr/	car
/ɔr/	horse
/ɛr/	their
/ʊr/	tourist
/ɪr/	ear

Diphthongs

/eɪ/	play, train
/aɪ/	ice, night
/ɔɪ/	employer, noisy
/aʊ/	house, download
/oʊ/	no, window

Consonants

/p/	push
/b/	bank
/t/	time
/d/	diary
/k/	carpet
/g/	big
/f/	surf
/v/	very
/θ/	thin
/ð/	that
/s/	sit
/z/	zero
/ʃ/	shine
/ʒ/	measure
/h/	hot
/w/	water
/ʧ/	chair
/ʤ/	joke
/m/	more
/n/	snow
/ŋ/	sing
/r/	ring
/l/	small
/y/	you

Grammar Review

Simple present — Unit 1

The *simple present* tense is used for habits and routines and to talk about facts.
I / You / We / They play football every Saturday.
The game starts at nine o'clock.
I don't eat meat.
My brother doesn't drive.

Present continuous — Unit 1

The *present continuous* tense is formed with the **simple present** form of **to be** + infinitive + **-ing**. The **-ing** form is the same for all persons, singular and plural.
I'm having lunch right now.
We're watching a DVD.
They aren't studying.
He isn't listening to music. He's talking on his phone.

The *present continuous* is used to talk about actions that are in progress at the time of speaking.

Present perfect — Unit 1

The *present perfect* tense is formed with the **present** tense of **have** + **past participle**:
They have finished their work.
I have seen the movie.

The past participle of regular verbs is formed like the *simple past,* by adding **-ed** to the infinitive of the verb.

The *present perfect* is used for past actions whose time is not specified.
Ben has left school. He's gone to China for a year.

The *present perfect* can be used with **ever** in an interrogative clause and with **never** in a negative clause:
***Have** you **ever skied**?*
*No, I've **never skied**.*

The *present perfect* can also express an action beginning in the past which is still continuing. It is often used with **for** (denoting a duration) or **since** (denoting the point in time when the action began):
*I've studied English **for** three years / **since** I was eleven.*

Past continuous

Unit 2

The *past continuous* tense is formed with the **past** tense of **to be** + infinitive + **-ing**:
What were you doing last night?
Paula was doing her homework, and I was playing a computer game.

The *past continuous* is often used with the *simple past*, to show that one action was in progress at a time in the past when another completed action (in the *simple past*) occurred.
I was having a shower when the phone rang.

It is also used with **while** or **as** to show that two actions in the past were happening at the same time.
While *I was waiting for the bus, I was listening to music on my MP3 player.*
I was thinking about summer vacation ***as*** *I was lying in bed.*

Past perfect

Unit 2

The *past perfect* tense is formed with the **past** tense of **have** + **past participle**:
He hadn't been at school for a few days, because he'd been sick.

The *past perfect* is used to show that one action in the past happened before another.
When I got to the concert, the band had started to play.
I had just finished my breakfast when I heard the doorbell ring.

Should / shouldn't and *ought / oughtn't*

Unit 3

Should and *shouldn't* are used to say what we think is a good idea, and to give advice. They are followed by the infinitive of the verb.
You should buy things online. It's so much easier.
You shouldn't tell anyone your bank account number.

We can also use *ought to* + the infinitive of the verb. We don't use *ought* as often as we use *should*.

Gerunds

Unit 3

A **gerund** is the **-ing** form of a verb. It can be used as the subject or as the object of a verb.
Shopping is my favorite hobby! (Subject)
I like ***swimming*** *and* ***playing*** *tennis.* (Object)

Talking about the future

Unit 4

Be going to / present continuous

We use **be going to** + infinitive to talk about future intentions.
I'm going to study drama when I'm in college.
What are you going to do when you arrive in Paris?
Shannon's going to design her own dress for the party.

The *present continuous* is also used to talk about the future. We usually use it to talk about fixed arrangements for the future.
I have a job in the summer. I'm working in a store.
We're having a barbeque on the beach on Saturday.

Future time clauses

Unit 4

As soon as, when, before, and *after* are often used to talk about actions in the future. In these phrases, the verb is in the present tense:
Please knock on the door before you come into the room.
I'll call you as soon as I get home.
When I graduate, I'm going to travel for a year.
Let's go get lunch after the class ends.

so / such

Unit 5

We can use *such* before a noun and *so* before an adjective to emphasize the quality of the noun or adjective. We can also talk about the result by adding *that* followed by a clause.
It was ***such*** *a nice day that we decided to have a picnic in the park.*
I was ***so*** *hot that I jumped right into the water.*
I'd never been into ***such*** *a wonderful building before.*
I was ***so*** *tired after our trip to the theme park.*

Phrasal verbs

Unit 5

Verbs followed by a preposition that cannot immediately be understood by looking at the individual words, are called *phrasal verbs*. The meaning of the verb often changes depending on the preposition following it:
take after = be similar to; **take up** = start a new hobby or activity; **turn into** = become;
turn off = use a switch to stop a radio or other device from operating
turn up = increase the volume;

The passive

Unit 6

The *simple present passive* has the following structure:
Subject + **simple present** of **be** (**not**) + **past participle**.

French is taught in most schools in Canada.

The *simple past passive* has the following structure:

Subject + **simple past** of **be** (**not**) + **past participle**.

The festival was held in June in Wisconsin.

make / let / be allowed to

Unit 6

Make + **object** + **infinitive** without "to" expresses obligation:
She ***made*** *the teacher really angry when she didn't listen.*
Let + **object** + **infinitive** without "to" is used to express permission to do a certain action:
My parents don't let me listen to music while I do my homework.

The passive form of *let* is the verb **to be** + **(past participle) allowed**. The past participle is the same for all persons, singular and plural.
Are you allowed to be out later than midnight?
Fran isn't allowed to wear makeup.
We aren't allowed to use cell phones in school.

Instruções de uso do CD-ROM

Instalação

Insira o CD-ROM **American MORE!** no compartimento de CD e siga na tela as instruções de instalação.
Se as instruções não aparecerem na tela, entre em *Meu Computador*, clique em D (ou no *drive* apropriado). Em seguida dê um duplo-clique no ícone *American More!* para iniciar a instalação.
Para usar o CD-ROM, dê um duplo-clique no atalho **American MORE!** criado na área de trabalho.

Conteúdo do CD-ROM

Exercícios interativos complementares para prática de vocabulário, gramática, pronúncia, leitura, compreensão oral e produção escrita, além de jogos divertidos. Clique em uma das unidades (Starter-12) e selecione uma das atividades para começar.

Configurações de sistema recomendadas

Windows 2000/XP/: 256MB RAM (mín. 512 MB)
Windows Vista/7: 1GB RAM (mín. 2GB)

Suporte

Para resolver problemas técnicos relacionados ao uso deste CD-ROM, acesse: www.cambridge.org/elt/multimedia/help

Termos e condições de uso para o **American MORE!** CD-ROM

1 Licença

(a) A Cambridge University Press e a Editora Ática concedem licença de uso desse CD-ROM (i) em um único computador para uma ou mais pessoas em momentos diferentes, ou (ii) para uma única pessoa em um ou mais computadores (contanto que o CD-ROM seja usado somente em um computador por vez e por apenas um usuário).

(b) Em relação ao conteúdo desse CD-ROM, o usuário não poderá: (i) copiar ou autorizar a cópia, (ii) traduzir, (iii) inverter a ordem ou alterar a estrutura, (iv) transferir, vender, delegar ou ceder qualquer parte, ou (v) disponibilizar em uma rede ou servidor.

2 Direitos Autorais

Todo conteúdo do CD-ROM é protegido pela lei de direito autoral e propriedade intelectual. O usuário adquire apenas o direito de uso do CD-ROM sem qualquer outro direito sobre seu conteúdo, expresso ou oculto, que não aqueles expressos na licença.

3 Obrigações

No âmbito jurídico, a Cambridge University Press e a Editora Ática não se responsabilizam por danos ou perdas de qualquer natureza decorrentes do uso desse produto ou de quaisquer erros e problemas no CD-ROM. Em todos os casos as obrigações das editoras se limitam ao valor real pago pelo produto.

Workbook 4 – Audio CD

Track	Time	Track	Time	Track	Time	Track	Time
1.	0'52"	12.	1'26"	23.	0'50"	34.	2'06"
2.	1'28"	13.	0'53"	24.	1'10"	35.	2'04"
3.	1'17"	14.	1'19"	25.	1'09"	36.	2'44"
4.	1'16"	15.	1'03"	26.	1'06"	37.	2'45"
5.	0'30"	16.	0'45"	27.	2'00"	38.	1'44"
6.	1'14"	17.	2'04"	28.	1'47"	39.	1'14"
7.	1'39"	18.	1'23"	29.	1'49"	40.	2'06"
8.	0'48"	19.	0'44"	30.	0'50"	41.	1'16"
9.	0'42"	20.	2'48"	31.	3'41"	42.	0'42"
10.	1'31"	21.	1'08"	32.	3'43"	43.	0'49"
11.	1'30"	22.	1'13"	33.	0'56"	44.	0'47"

Total Duration: 64min50s